THE RUSSIAN CLERGY.

Translated from the French of

FATHER GAGARIN, S.J.

BY

CH. DU GARD MAKEPEACE, M.A.

AMS PRESS, INC.
NEW YORK

Reprinted from the edition of 1872, London
First AMS EDITION published 1970
Manufactured in the United States of America

International Standard Book Number: 0-404-02666-4

Library of Congress Catalog Card Number: 70-131035

AMS PRESS, INC.
NEW YORK, N.Y. 10003

AUTHOR'S PREFACE

TO THE ENGLISH EDITION.

——•——

SINCE the following pages were first written and published in French, many attempts have been made in Russia to effect reforms in the clergy, such as the abolition of caste, the improvement of schools, and the granting to bishops and priests a little more independence.

We by no means call in question the good intentions that prompted these reforms; but we must remark, that some have been decreed on paper without bringing about any sensible and real change, and the others leave untouched the foundations and roots of the evil we have sought to disclose. In every case, many years must elapse before any change can be felt as their result. After these reforms, the clergy is still a caste separated from the rest of the nation, and the Church is still in absolute dependence on the State. The causes of this situation remain; we do not see what we have to consider as changed.

That there may be in Russia a certain tendency to move towards the separation of Church and State, we do not deny; nor do we dispute that in time this tendency of men's minds may lead to radical changes in the mutual relations of the Russian Government and the official Church; but, hitherto, nothing has been done in this direction, and this unfortunate Church, attacked on the one side by the *Raskol,* and on the other by *Nihilism,* seems, notwithstanding all appearances of prosperity, destined speedily to perish. Strangely should we deceive ourselves if we failed to see that these twin plagues of the contemporaneous Russian Church have developed, and continue to develop themselves solely in consequence of the absorption of the Church by the State; and until a remedy shall have been applied to this fundamental evil, reformers will have accomplished nothing.

Paris, April 1872.

TRANSLATOR'S PREFACE.

———

HAVING, at an esteemed friend's request, read the original of this work, *Le Clergé Russe*, I concurred in his opinion that the graphic picture it contained of Russian ecclesiastical life and organisation was so instructive, especially in the present transition state of ecclesiastical thought and feeling in England, that to unveil it to English eyes would render service, albeit but humble, to the sacred cause of truth and progress.

Inasmuch as the Author, whose work I have translated, is a living Catholic Father as well as an historical writer of repute, I, a Protestant, felt bound, especially after being favoured with the Author's consent to the translation, to allow him, by a very faithful rendering of the original, to speak not only as an historian, but also as a Catholic.

Two works of merit have recently issued from the press in this country treating on subjects closely connected with that of this work; and from the pens of writers whose careful observation and wide research invest their works with interest and entitle them to authority.

The one is, *The Patriarch and the Tsar,—The Replies of the humble Nicon, by the mercy of God Patriarch* (of Moscow), &c. (London, Trübner, 1871), in which the Author, W. Palmer, M.A., of Magdalen College, Oxford, specially vindicates the character of the most eminent among the sufferers for spiritual independence in Russia. The other, *The Pope of Rome and the Popes of the Oriental Orthodox Church* (London, Longmans, 1871), in which the Rev. Father Tondini, Barnabite, so conclusively demonstrates the enslavement of the Russian episcopate, and so clearly traces it to its source, the will of the autocrat, as surely to deter all Anglicans from looking for union eastwards.

That, with these two, the present work, by widening the field of facts to the eye of the observing, may contribute to correct errors inherited from the past, and to form universally sounder principles of ecclesiastical polity in the future, is the earnest wish doubtless of the Author, and certainly of the

TRANSLATOR.

London, April 3, 1872.

CONTENTS.

———◆———

THE RUSSIAN CLERGY.

INTRODUCTION.

THE accession of the Emperor Alexander II.
to the throne of Russia inaugurated a new era
for that vast empire. Since that event the serfs
have been emancipated; the introduction of
trial by jury with an oral and public procedure
has completely reorganised the administration
of justice; and territorial institutions have laid
the first foundations of self-government. With
these important and salutary reforms, however,
we have not to be occupied. We confine ourselves to a single observation. Those inveter-
ate abuses could not be touched without the
discovery of others, and reforms already effected
could not but open the path to new ones. Among
those yet to be accomplished, one of the most
important concerns the clergy and the organisa-

tion of the Russian Church. During the reign of the Emperor Nicholas public opinion was little interested in the situation of the clergy. In connection with it many abuses were known to exist, but their correction seemed to be a matter of little importance. For some thirty years M. André Mouravieff alone devoted his pen to this subject; but his chief object was to throw a veil over disorders unfortunately too real: he denied the abuses, not combated them. It is not so now. The laity, through the press, are allowed to make frequent attacks more or less clear and direct against the Russian clergy, and the latter reply. A considerable number of journals and ecclesiastical reviews exist, the chief work of which is to defend the clergy, but which, however, from time to time call loudly for reform. This publicity is quite insufficient, because of the very narrow limits imposed on the liberty of the press. When a question arises of abuses existing in the administrative order, a sufficiently great latitude is accorded to the journals. By the aid of rhetorical precautions they were recently able to make a breach in the fundamental principles of Christianity and of social order; but were checked when their efforts were directed against the clergy and church organisation. Everything touching on matters of this kind being subjected to ecclesiastical censure, it is almost impossible to carry on discussion on this ground. In this embarrassment recourse was had to the foreign press. In 1858 a very remarkable pamphlet was published at Paris on the condition of the country clergy of Russia.* It contained harrowing details on the abuses existing in the administration of the dioceses, and in the establishments for the education and formation of the clergy. This pamphlet produced in Russia a prodigious effect. Although its author took care to conceal his name, it was soon known that he was a poor priest of the diocese of Tver, named Belustin. The Synod was much irritated, and about to make the unfortunate writer feel the weight of its anger, when the intervention of M. Bajanoff, the Emperor's confessor, sheltered him from all persecution.

It cannot be doubted that this publication had some influence on a decision taken by the Synod at the beginning of 1859. By the organ of the Chief Procurator of the Synod† all the bishops were invited to send to this assembly their opinion on the condition of the ecclesiastical schools, and the means of improving them.

* Описаніе сельскаго духовенства—русскій заграничный Сборникъ, iv. Paris, Frank, 1858.

† See, for the functions of the Chief Procurator, farther on, chap. v.

The bishops requested the advice of the rectors and superiors of the seminaries: these consulted the directors and professors; the result was a vast inquiry, which in a few months placed the Synod in possession of a voluminous correspondence. A special commission was appointed to sift it, and to draw up a scheme of regulation for the seminaries. This was laid aside, we know not why, and replaced by another commission composed of two rectors, four secular priests, and two laymen, under the presidency of a member of the episcopate.

In 1862 this commission presented to the Synod its scheme, which was printed in 1863, with the objections made by the two laymen, the *procès verbaux* of the commission, and several other papers. The whole work was sent to the bishops, who were obliged to open a new inquiry. Meanwhile, there appeared at Leipsic anonymously another work, on the condition of the clerical schools in Russia.* From day to day the ecclesiastical question filled a larger place in the attention of the public and of the government; and on the 28th of June 1862 the Emperor caused a proposal to be made in the Synod for an inquiry as to the means of ameliorating the condition of the

---

* Объ устройствѣ духовныхъ училищъ въ россіи. Leipzig, Wagner, 1863. 8vo.

clergy. A new commission was appointed, under the presidency of the Metropolitan of St. Petersburg. It was composed of all the members of the Synod, the ministers of the Interior, of the Domains, and of Police, of the Chief Procurator of the Synod, and the Director-General of the Ecclesiastical Schools, Prince Ouroussoff, to whom were joined Count de Tolstoy, the Chamberlain Batuchkoff, and M. Demontovig.

On January 17th, 1863, a paper of questions was addressed to the bishops. In April of the same year sub-commissions were formed in each diocese, composed of the diocesan, the Provincial Governor, and the Director of Domains. These sub-commissions addressed themselves, it may be said, to everybody for information; and the result was the creation in 1864 for each parish of a species of churchwarden committee, which were also bound to seek the means for improving the condition of the clergy, *i.e.* for augmenting their incomes.

We will not examine if the wide scope given to this inquiry did not conceal the intent to mar the work of reform. It is quite certain that this great question was set down in the *orders for the day*, and the government itself allowed that something must be done. The Press was thereby encouraged, and set

itself more vigorously to point out the abuses
it noticed in the clergy and in their schools.
To these attacks replies came from different
quarters, but seem to have produced but little
effect.

If one compares the course adopted by the
Russian government, when it took in hand the
emancipation of the peasantry, and that which
it pursues on the present question, there will
be no difficulty in becoming convinced that
this double inquiry into the situation of the
clergy and the ecclesiastical schools, must terminate in results much more important than
one would at first sight suppose. There is
among the Russian clergy such a mass of
abuses, and these so interlaced one with another, that the subject cannot be touched without revealing the necessity of a radical reform,
and of a new organisation in the Church itself.
The first thing to be done is to *establish* the
existence of the evil, then to find the remedy,
and to apply it. Without doubt this question
bristles with difficulties far otherwise serious
than all those which the government has
hitherto undertaken to resolve : but on the
other hand, the necessity of destroying the
abuses and effecting reforms is so evident that
it is impossible to draw back. It must therefore be admitted that reform will take place ;

but how, and by whom, will it be brought
about? Will the Russian Church be left to
achieve this great work herself,—will she be
allowed to assemble in council, or rather, will
the government take it in hand?

'Tis very natural that the Russian clergy
should display little eagerness to allow themselves to be reformed by the civil power, and
it is not for us to reproach them; but we must
say that the resistance they can oppose is by
no means formidable. The government, herein
agreeing with public opinion, seems convinced
that reform would not take place if the task of
effecting it were abandoned to the clergy. The
efforts which the Synod or the bishops would
make to be intrusted with this task would be
considered only as a means of shelving the
question. Besides, the Russian clergy have
not strength enough to contend with the government. Long ago it renounced all power
of originating action, and abdicated all independence. Of the numerous causes of its weakness there is one which it concerns us to point
out.

The Russian clergy is divided; in its bosom
are two parties hostile the one to the other;
the secular, and the regular clergy. The latter
body, which consists exclusively of the monks
of St. Basil, is in Russia vulgarly designated

the *Black clergy*,* probably because it alone
uniformly wears vestments of that colour. By
opposition the secular clergy are called the
White clergy.† These designations being short
and expressive, we deem it expedient to adopt
them.

The history of the Catholic Church reveals
traces of a rivalry between the secular and
regular clergy; but this in its most lively
manifestations cannot be compared with the
profound hatred with which the secular clergy
of Russia regard the regular. This state of
things is due to several causes. Let us first
point to the publication of an important work
which treats on this question *ex professo*.

There has just appeared at Leipsic, in the
Russian language, a book entitled, *Of the
White and Black Clergy of Russia*.‡ The author, who has not deemed it expedient to publish his name, shows himself the violent enemy
of the Black clergy. It is true that he is not
very tender towards the *White* clergy; that he
unveils many grave abuses, the reform of
which he energetically demands. But in acting thus, he does not show himself the enemy
of these, and indeed 'tis *their* cause he pro-

---

* Черное духовенство.   † Бѣлое духовенство.

‡ О православномъ бѣломъ и черномъ духовенствѣ въ россіи. Leipzig, Wagner, 1866.

fesses to serve. The book is at once a rude attack on the Black clergy, and a programme of the reforms wished by the White. It is impossible for us to adopt the point of view of this anonymous writer; but his work contains revelations so curious and important, it touches almost all sides of the question with so much vigour, that one reads it with the liveliest interest.

The situation of the Russian clergy being but imperfectly known out of Russia, we have thought it expedient to profit by this publication in calling the attention of our readers to this subject. Moreover, it seemed to us to belong to a Catholic pen to correct the erroneous ideas of the author, to indicate the real causes of the abuses, and the path in which must be sought the solution of the problem.

For the sake of order we will successively treat—1st, of the *White* clergy; 2d, of the *Black* clergy; 3d, of the Ecclesiastical Schools; 4th, of the Episcopate; and 5th, of the Government of the Church.

CHAPTER I.

THE WHITE CLERGY.

In the Latin Church celibacy is obligatory on all clerks in Holy Orders, beginning with the subdeacons. In the East a less rigorous discipline has long prevailed. There, as in the Latin Church,* once let a man enter Holy Orders, he can no longer marry; the Sacrament of the Order is an impediment dirimant to marriage† in the East as well as in the West. But if a married man present himself for ordination he is not rejected, and is permitted to keep his wife. This custom is so rooted in Eastern manners, that when Eastern Churches

---

* The Orders of the Roman Church, unlike those of the English, are divided into Major and Minor; the latter embracing the Acolytus, Ostiarius (the door-keeper), Lector (reader), and Exorcista (exorciser). The Major include the subdeacon, deacon, and priest with bishop. These last form the different degrees of the Sacrament of Order, are called holy, and cannot be repeated. Obligatory celibacy applies from the subdeacon upwards. (*Trans.*)

† The *impedimenta* to marriage are, in the language of the canon law, either *impedientia* or *dirimentia*. The former are those circumstances that make the marriage unlawful, but which, when it has been contracted, do not affect its validity; the latter are those which render the marriage not only unlawful, but invalid.

have reëntered the communion of the Catholic Church and recognised the authority of the Pope, the Holy See has not exacted from them conformity to the ecclesiastical law of celibacy. It cannot be said that this condescension to ancient customs involves any serious inconveniences. I have seen close at hand Maronite priests, who are generally married; it is not rare to find among them virtuous men, excellent Christians, and even very good priests. But it is certain that the population of the Lebanon is found amid conditions quite exceptional. The inhabitants of a Maronite village would not understand a curé not being chosen by themselves, and would have much difficulty in taking as curé a stranger to their village. When the cure is vacant, they assemble, and make choice of some peasant, some good father of a family, a good Christian, who has probably never dreamt of being clothed with an ecclesiastical status. They present him to the bishop, and if the testimonies in his behalf are satisfactory, if he can read the Syriac characters, he is sent to pass three weeks in a convent. He there learns to say mass, to ad-

---

The union of a Catholic with a non-Catholic Christian, without previous dispensation, is an instance of the former (*impedientia*); the union of persons within the second degree of consanguinity is an instance of the latter (*dirimentia*). (*Trans.*)

minister the sacraments; and when deemed just
sufficiently instructed, is ordained, and returns
to his village to take possession of his cure.

Amid these populations, simple and full of
faith, such an organisation is possible; perhaps,
considering the state of the country, it would
be difficult to substitute a better. In other
circumstances this would be manifestly different. We shall presently see that the organisation of the married clergy of Russia has no
resemblance whatever to that we have just
sketched. Among the Maronites themselves
circumstances are being modified, and in proportion as the people lose their simplicity, it
becomes a necessity to reduce the number of
married priests. The bishops, doubtless, sometimes have trouble in resisting the pressing
applications made to them; but, in many cases,
it is necessary to know how to oppose an un-
shakeable firmness to all solicitation.

From what we have just said, it results
that, in given circumstances, priests being
fathers of families can indeed administer the
sacraments of baptism and marriage, conduct
burials, celebrate the holy mass, chant the
offices, and hear a certain number of confessions, especially at Easter. But it is not difficult to understand that, absorbed by the care
of their households, by the education and

settlement of their children, they do not bring to the exercise of their sacred ministry the same zeal, devotion, and self-denial as those priests who are free from such cares. Take, for example, the case of hearing the confession of a person dying of some contagious disease : the priest celibate will go, as a soldier goes to meet fire ; but the father of a family—will he always have the courage to expose the lives of his children ? Nay, we ought not to expect to find in a married priest the same disinterestedness as in a celibate priest. A man will much more easily encounter privations when he alone will be the sufferer, than when he must impose them on all those who are dearest to him.

To go no farther, it is evident that a Church with no other clergy than married priests would present a gap, and would not be in a normal condition. Even in all the Eastern Churches, side by side with the married are found unmarried clergy—the monks. It seems to be admitted in these countries that, with exceptions more or less frequent, a celibate priest, that he may not be exposed to deplorable falls, needs to be surrounded by all the aids the religious life affords; we mean, the probation of the novitiate, the salutary yoke of vows, the observance of rules, the monastic life, the vigilance of superiors, and the most multiplied exercises of piety. There are, then, in the East, as in the West, two orders of clergy; the one secular, the other regular. In the Latin Church both are bound by the law of celibacy; in the Oriental the secular clergy are in general married, and with few exceptions all the celibate priests make profession of the religious life at the same time.

One very important consequence of this organisation is, that, in the East, most, if not all, of the bishops are drawn from the regular clergy. Following the discipline universally admitted in the Eastern as in the Western Church, the bishops are bound to celibacy. If, then, the clergy are married, the bishops must be taken from among the monks.

It is easy to understand that this organisation gives to the regular clergy in the Eastern Church a preponderating influence and authority; by the very force of things, the secular clergy is, with regard to the regular, in an inferior and subordinate position. Let us not forget the fundamental cause—the root of their inferiority—their marriage.

Let us return to the Russian Church. In it the distinction between the two classes of clergy, the Black and the White (regular and secular), has always existed; but we do not see that in the past there has been any strife between these classes. This fact is easily accounted for. The situation of the White clergy had formerly in Russia more than one feature of resemblance to that of the Maronite clergy, as above sketched. All instruction, intelligence, and vitality in the clergy belonged to the monks. The married clergy had no kind of study; the accomplishment of their functions, the care of their households, and the necessities of life, wholly absorbed them; it never even entered their minds to contest any matter with the monks, who ruled everywhere. The anonymous author of the book *On the White and Black Clergy* has vainly laboured to discover, before the creation of the Synod, traces of the hostility by which these two clerical classes are to-day mutually animated. All he has been able to cite are one or two insignificant facts.

But the condition of the Russian Church is no longer what it was in the time of the old tsars. Peter I. did not confine himself to suppressing the Patriarchate and replacing it by the Synod. He overturned the organisation of the Church to its foundations; he effected in it a *true revolution.** His successors have

---

* On the liability of the Russian Church to revolutions, see chap. iii. of Tondini's *The Pope of Rome and the Popes,* &c. (*Trans.*)

continued his work; the old canonical law has
been swept away by the *Spiritual Regulation*,*
and the old customs by a multitude of ukases.
Neither the government of the dioceses, nor
the mode of collation to bishoprics and cures,
nor the conditions of the monastic life, nor
theological instruction,—nothing escaped the
blind brusque rage for reform which planted
more abuses than it uprooted. In the midst
of so many subversions, the situation of the
White clergy could not fail to be profoundly
altered. So, indeed, it happened. It underwent a radical transformation. From all time
there had been in Russia priests who were
married and had families; but their children
were perfectly free not to embrace the ecclesiastical state, and the clergy were recruited
from all classes of society. To-day the son of
a priest or deacon is destined by his birth to
enter the clerical ranks; it is an obligation
from which he is not permitted to withdraw
himself. The son of a nobleman, of a merchant, of a citizen, of a peasant, who wished
to be admitted to Holy Orders, would meet
with insurmountable obstacles.†

It is this strange and deplorable state of

* On the 'Spiritual Regulation' an interesting analysis is given
farther on, at chap. v.
† This applies only to the White clergy.

things which the *Moscow Gazette**[*]* lately designated as ' Leviteism,' and which it pointed out
as one of the plagues of the Russian Church.
Nothing is more true. Peter I. and his successors, with the complicity of the Synod, made
of the clergy an hereditary and close corporation—a caste. It is allowable to suppose that
they did not propose to themselves such a result; but still it is necessary to see by what
series of measures, by what chain of usurpa-
tions and iniquities, they arrived at it.

The creation of seminaries was the first
cause of it. The ignorance of the clergy being complained of, a decree was issued for the
founding of ecclesiastical schools. These remained deserted. The clergy were then *ordered*
to send their children there; and as these did
not go by any means willingly, they were taken
there by force—sometimes even *loaded with
chains*. Here we see an application of the principle of *gratuitous and compulsory instruction*.

The ukases of Alexander I., published in
1808 and 1814, declare that all the children
of clerks, from the age of six years to eight,
are at the disposition of the Ecclesiastical School
department.†

---

* Московскія Вѣдомости (daily newspaper published at Moscow,
the chief editor of which is the celebrated Mr. Katkoff).

† О правосл. бѣл. и черн. духов, tom. ii. p. 355.

At the same period military colonies were organised, and the children of soldiers were incorporated with the army under the name of Cantonists. It was a veritable application of serfdom. If peasants were attached to the cultivation of the soil, the offspring of priests and deacons could well be so to the service of the altar. When once the Synod or the State had been at the expense of the children's education, it seemed just that they should wish to be indemnified for it. The seminarists had no other prospect than that of entering the ecclesiastical state. In order to pursue any other career, they needed a special permission, which was very difficult to obtain, and almost always refused.

When by this means a number of ecclesiastics in proportion to the disposable places was secured, it would seem that the prevailing rigour could have been relaxed. Nothing of the kind; but, in order to put the children of the clergy in safety from an unpleasant competition, obstacles were multiplied to other classes of society gaining access to the sanctuary. In this way the creation of an hereditary clergy was in a very short time successful. The sovereigns decreed these things, their ministers proposed them, the members of the Synod sanctioned them, and the bishops witnessed them, but said nothing. We should be glad to find in history any trace of a protest, to catch the cry of one indignant conscience. Hitherto we have met with nothing of the sort.

This is not all: marriage before ordination was licensed; it was now made obligatory. It seems, at least, that the seminarist, obliged to be married before receiving Holy Orders, must be free to choose his companion. But priests and deacons have daughters for whom settlements must be found : hence arose a prohibition from marrying out of the caste. There are some bishops who even do not tolerate their clergy marrying out of their diocesan clergy.

The principle of inheritance once laid down, its consequences flow spontaneously. For example, here is a country curé who has built a house on land belonging to the Church. He dies. His successor wishes to take possession of the parsonage; but the son or daughter of the deceased claims the house, which forms part of his inheritance, and a law-suit follows. The case has presented itself more than once; the legislator has interfered; and, to reconcile the interests in conflict, an ukase of January 22d, 1768, permitted the diocesan authority to assure the vacant cure to him who shall espouse the heiress of the deceased priest, or to reserve it for the son yet under age. Here, then, is inheritance as applied to the collation to cures; here is seen how the body of legislative enactments issued by Catherine II. and Alexander I. ended in making of the clergy an actual close corporation, an hereditary caste. Can one, after this, speak of a vocation? Can one expect that, in a clergy recruited in this fashion, there will be many priests penetrated with the sacredness of their status, acquitting themselves of their duties with devotion, zeal, and self-denial? It is a trade, and, moreover, a trade which has not been freely chosen. Good reason has M. Katkoff to ask for the destruction of *Leviteism!*

There is in Russia a sect called Nihilists, who deny everything and believe nothing. The existence of God, the immortality of the soul, the future state, the fundamental bases of society, marriage, property—they reject everything. Nihilism is rapidly spreading in the universities; but if we may believe the *Moscow Gazette*, it has committed still greater ravages in the seminaries. Can any one figure to himself a Nihilist clothed with the sacerdotal character? We well know that these gentlemen have a profound aversion to the ecclesiastical state, and that in presence of their energetic remonstrances it is absolutely necessary to allow them to embrace another profession.

Crowds of young persons are also now seen deserting the seminaries and academies for the benches of universities, or to enter on the career of instruction. But is not this fact itself a clear proof of something vicious in the hereditary organisation of the Russian clergy?

The hatred of the *White* clergy for the *Black* dates from the day when it became a caste. The frequenting the seminaries contributed much of it; but this feeling was developed *pari passu* with their *esprit de corps*. Besides the diocesan seminaries, there are in the Russian Church at Petersburg, Moscow, Kieff, and Kasan, what are called ecclesiastical academies. These are houses for high studies, kinds of Faculties of Theology. Hither are sent the best scholars from all the seminaries, and hence issue forth the *élite* of the whole clergy. Usually, the youths arrive there without having taken on themselves any engagement; but, in the course of their studies, and especially in the last year, there are a certain number of them who adopt the *religious* habit. These see the path to ecclesiastical honours open at once before them. On leaving the academy, they rarely fail to be at once nominated prefects of studies in a seminary; they afterwards become superiors, rectors, priors, archimandrites, bishops. Those of their fellow-students who preferred to marry and remain among the secular clergy, can aspire to no such advancement. They have before them no other future than the hope of obtaining a cure, or rather of becoming embassy chaplains. The number of these latter, however, is very limited.

It remains, then, that, with very rare exceptions, power, fortune, honourable distinctions, are on the side of the monastic habit. The pupils of the academy who have preferred to be married soon find themselves burdened with a numerous family; their incomes are insufficient, and they have little hope of improving their position. On the other hand, the diocesan government in Russia is, it is true, confided to the bishops; but these exercise their authority only through the medium of a venal and teasing bureaucracy, from which the curés have much to suffer. It is, therefore, not at all astonishing that the rivalry begun on the benches at school should do naught but grow.

It is not only rivalry and jealousy which separate the two classes of the clergy; there is a sufficiently great difference in their modes of viewing things.

If one said that the White clergy have Protestant tendencies, and the Black clergy Roman, he would not express himself exactly; but, in comparing the Russian Church to the Anglican, one would say that the White clergy somewhat resemble the low-church, and the Black the high-church party. The former has a Presbyterian cast, whilst the latter defends the rights of the hierarchy.

What we have just advanced can give an idea of the war these two classes are waging. The Black clergy seems master of all the important positions; people do not forget to cry aloud that it is all-powerful, that it oppresses the White clergy. In fact, the bishops and the monks are reduced to defend themselves, and do so ill enough; whilst their adversaries have boldly taken the offensive, and will doubtless stop only when they shall have reduced the Black clergy to nothing. They have already won important positions. The embassy chaplains were, down to the beginning of the present century, taken from among the monks, a practice affording great advantages. To-day all, or nearly all, are secular priests. It is the same with the military chaplains. The Emperor's confessor is a married priest, and a member of the Synod, as also the Chaplain-in-chief of the Army and Navy. Hence the

White clergy are assured of two voices in the bosom of the assembly which governs the Russian Church—two very influential voices, before which the majority is often compelled to bow. These conquests do not satisfy its ambition, nor will it think it has gained anything until admitted to the ranks of the Episcopate. This is the aim of all its efforts; but it is a point not easily carried. Never have married bishops been seen in the Russian Church. To introduce such an innovation, it were necessary to trample under foot all tradition, the popular sentiment, the canons of the Church; but nothing can stay the prosecution of the White clergy's designs, and it is possible it may ultimately reach the goal. To accustom the mind to such a result, permission is beginning to be given to some married priests to wear the mitre. It adorns the brow of two members of the Synod, of M. Wassilieff, ex-chaplain to the Russian Embassy at Paris, and of three or four others.

At the head of this party public opinion places M. Bajanoff, the Emperor's confessor. The opposite party was headed by the late Mgr. Filaret, Metropolitan of Moscow,* whose old age

* Born in 1782, Filaret died November 18th, 1867. See *Biographie Universelle* of Didot (Paris). His death was accompanied with mournful incidents, which may be found in contemporary correspondence.

was attended by the universal esteem of the whole empire, and whose personal influence in the Church whilst living was undeniable. But he once dead, the Black clergy found itself deprived of its firmest supporter in the resistance it is opposing to the enterprises of the White.

It is the Bajanoff party which has brought to light the works we cited above. They are published abroad, because the ecclesiastical censorship exercised by the monks would by no means permit them to pass. But the government has no motive to hinder their circulation, and we can believe they regard them without displeasure.

Generally, it may be said that, in the conflict it is waging with the Black clergy, the White has on its side the government, the opinion of people (ever increasing in number) who have lost all religious conviction, and the majority of the journals. The great strength of the opposite party is in the people, and in the fear that exists that the ranks of the Staroveres* would thicken, should too flagrant innovations be attempted.

---

* *Staroveres* (Старовѣры), literally 'old believers.' This denomination is applied to that large portion of the Russian dissenters which, while retaining the dogmas of the Russian Orthodox Church, repudiate the jurisdiction of the holy Synod. The origin of the Russian dissenters, known generally under the name *Raskol*

No; if the men in whose hands are the destinies of the Russian Church will listen to the counsels of wisdom, that is not the end towards which they will direct their efforts. The most important and urgent of all reforms is, the abrogation of the measures which have resulted in making the clergy an hereditary caste. Let the entrance of the sanctuary be open to all those, whatever their origin, whom a true vocation leads to the service of its altars; let the children of ecclesiastics, when they have no priestly vocation, be free to embrace what career they wish; and the greater part of the abuses which are now complained of will be destroyed in their very root.

To achieve this result, it is necessary that the seminaries and ecclesiastical schools should undergo a complete transformation. Ecclesiastics must no longer be constrained to send their children thither, nor the children of other classes excluded therefrom. It is equally urgent to destroy all those abuses which the principle

---

(schism, Russ. расколъ), dates from the great Patriarch Nicon's correction of the liturgical books (1660). Of this great victim to the conflicts between the civil and ecclesiastical powers, who is the embodied idea of that independence which it is time the Russian clergy wrested from the Tsar, see the valuable work of W. Palmer, Esq., M.A. Oxon, *The Patriarch and the Tsar—The Replies of the humble Nicon*, &c. (London, Trübner and Co. 1871.) (*Tr.*)

of inheritance and the pecuniary arrangements have introduced into the collations to cures. It is necessary that in every parish there be close to the church a parsonage for the abode of the curé. This parsonage being the property of the parish, the curé should have the usufruct of it so long as he shall be invested with his functions; he should be at liberty to dispose of it neither by sale nor by will; and at his death, or when from any cause whatever he should cease from his functions, neither he nor his family should have any claim on this property. It is also necessary that the mode of collation to cures should be so regulated that venality and corruption may be completely shut out. And, farther, that the young people of both sexes, children of ecclesiastics, should be perfectly free to marry outside their caste. The author of the book *On the White and Black Clergy* insists very strongly on this point, and with good reason. By what right do you impose on the daughter of an ecclesiastic the obligation to become the wife of a priest or of a deacon? The inclination of her heart, social proprieties, the blessing of her parents, cannot these point out to her elsewhere a happy path of life? Why, on his side, should not the son of a priest find a companion in the family of a decent *employé*, of one of the lower gentry, of a rich peasant, of a citizen, of a tradesman?

By a necessary consequence, the houses exclusively appropriated to the education of the daughters of ecclesiastics have no *raison d'être*. Here, again, must be destroyed the spirit of caste; no one must be compelled to send his daughters to these establishments, no one excluded from them on the score of birth; nor, above all, the establishments themselves made nurseries exclusively destined to furnish wives for the clergy. It is useless to insist on truths so evident. How can we, without profound astonishment, see upright souls and sound minds of our own day conceiving the odd idea of forming boarding-schools intended to educate priests' daughters to become the wives of priests! Surely the spirit of caste must have taken the deepest root in the country, when foundations so strange have not only excited no surprise, but even met with sympathy.

Let us now pass to another consideration, and say a few words on ecclesiastical celibacy.

We have seen that the Holy See does not impose it on the Oriental clergy, and we by no means intend to show ourselves more exacting than the Holy See. Besides, we willingly recognise that, in the actual circumstances, and perhaps for yet a long period, there would be more inconveniences than advantages in rendering celibacy obligatory on the Russian clergy. This, however, is a point on which we cannot possibly insist. If the discipline of the Oriental Church permits married persons to be admitted to Holy Orders without imposing the obligation of separating from their wives, it does not follow that marriage should be *a necessary condition* to ordination. Canon law never prescribed it in the Greek Church, and, down to the present time, the practice of the different Oriental Churches on this point is in agreement with canon law.

In Russia alone has the custom prevailed of requiring the marriage of all who are to be ordained among the secular clergy. But even in Russia this custom, how general soever, has not the force of law. A recent fact proves this. Some years ago, Mgr. Filaret ordained as priest a M. Gorski, a celibate but not a monk. The legality of this act is not to be doubted; but so strongly rooted is the contrary custom, that in the whole Russian Church not a single bishop would be found to imitate Mgr. Filaret's example. We have not heard that this prelate has himself followed his own lead, and made a second ordination in the same circumstances. However, it cannot be doubted that among the young men who finish their theological studies in the ecclesiastical academies, there are some who would ask nothing better than to be ordained while remaining unmarried, and making no profession of the monastic life. By what right is it required of them to clothe themselves with the bonds of marriage? This is one more question asking for immediate settlement, which can be only on the side of liberty.

How can one help seeing the immense advantages of creating a *secular celibate clergy*, holding a middle place between the *married* and the *regular?* We would not begin by giving to such priests country cures. Why not employ them in seminaries and in the academies? Let *some* of these establishments be confided to monks—there is no difficulty in this; but why should they *all* be? That the married clergy should be excluded from these houses is perfectly understood; but why extend exclusion to secular celibate priests? I go farther. When a celibate priest shall have arrived at a certain age, and given proofs of solid virtue, he should be set over an important parish in a large town. This result once obtained, nothing would prevent the settlement near him of younger priests equally celibate, who should live with him, and, profiting by his experience, exercise themselves in sacerdotal duties.

After having passed a few years under the direction of older priests, these young men could be set over less important parishes. Finally, from the ranks of such clergy bishops could be chosen, and the unmixed advantage gained of not recruiting the Episcopate exclusively from the monks.

The existence of this intermediate clergy would contribute much to extinguish the hostility which now reigns between the White and Black clergy, and it would at the same time be a new barrier against *Leviteism.* In a word, on whatever side one views the question, one sees only advantage in breaking away from a routine which nothing justifies, and in leaving aspirants to the priesthood free to choose between marriage and celibacy. The author of the book *On the White and Black Clergy* would wish that priests who become widowers might be authorised to contract a new marriage. We need not stop to point out that this would be a very grave infraction of ecclesiastical law, an innovation involving the most serious inconveniences. Without speaking of the prescriptions of the canon law, who does not see the very great difference between a married man clothed with the sacerdotal character, and a priest in whom mothers and their daughters might see a *match,* or who himself, among the

young people with whom his functions bring
him in contact, might look for one to whom
he could offer his heart and hand, and pay his
courtship? In such a situation, what would
become of confession? Let us pass on.

Of all the reforms which the sad condition
of the White clergy claims, the only one which
is discussed with a little heat in the press, the
only one to which the public and the government seem to attach any value, has for its
object to ameliorate their situation; in other
terms, to increase their revenues. In our eyes
this reform has not the importance which they
attach to it. There are many others more
urgent; but yet it is necessary to say a few
words on this.

Let us begin by showing the pecuniary resources of the White clergy. Adopting our
author's figures, these are the results we arrive at. For greater clearness, we convert the
rouble into its near equivalent, 3*s.* 2*d.* We
do not take into calculation the stipend allotted
to the chaplains of prisons, hospitals, hospices,
gymnasiums, schools, &c. In speaking of chaplains for gymnasiums, colleges, schools, &c.,
we conform our language to French usage; it
would be more exact to say catechists. Our
author recognises that in general all these ecclesiastics are liberally paid. The less favoured

fulfil, at the same time, other functions. We are then concerned only with the parochial clergy properly so called. Here are their incomes:

1st. Perpetual foundations, with obligation to pray for the departed. These are in state funds, and yield a return of 4 per cent. Their amount is not stated.

2d. Houses and properties belonging to parishes, and chiefly in towns. Under this head there is a revenue of 100,000*l.*

3d. Provision paid by the treasury, 600,000*l.*

4th. Contributions of the parishioners, comprising the *casual* also. Our author estimates that they should amount to 4,000,000*l.*

That makes a total of 4,700,000*l.*, to be distributed among 36,000 parishes, giving for each parish 131*l.* 12*s.*

In Russia the clergy of a parish regularly consists of a priest, a deacon, and two clerics discharging the duties of sacristan, beadle, ringer, lector, &c.

The total revenue is distributed thus: to the priest, the half; to the deacon, the quarter; and the remainder to the two clerics. The income of the curés must, then, be rated at 65*l.* 16*s.* But, as for 36,000 priests there are only 12,444 deacons and 63,421 clerics, the incomes of the priests are increased by a fifth, and reach, on an average, 83*l.* More-

over, each parish possesses a minimum of 33
hectares; which gives, according to the same
calculations, an average of 20 hectares, the
usufruct of which belongs to the curé. The
quantity of land assigned to the clergy in many
parishes is much more considerable. In provinces so fertile, the true granary of Russia,
known under the name of the Black Lands, it
is not rare that the curé's share rises to 30,
40, and 60 hectares.* In such a parish, on the
banks of the Oka, the meadows assigned to the
clergy yield for the priest's share 40*l*. Elsewhere the Church possesses considerable woods
and forests; but this is an uncommon case.

Our author maintains no less that the
condition of the Russian clergy is profoundly
miserable. This is hardly credible; but, supposing it to be true, it is in lessening the expenses, not in increasing the receipts, that the
remedy for the evil is to be sought. If the
priests were not married, this result might be
easily attained. Suppose the curé unmarried,
and you will recognise that the state and the
parishes largely supply all his wants. I shall
perhaps be answered, that the discipline of the
Russian Church permits the Russian curé to
marry. I grant it; but if he profit by the

* In the governments of the centre are found parishes possessing 100, 200, or even 1000 hectares.

authorisation that is given him, and incur pecuniary trouble thereby, he can blame none but himself. I do not see that the faithful should be obliged to provide for the maintenance of his wife and children. And the less so, because, if celibate, he would have more time to devote to them, would catechise the children, instruct the ignorant, visit the sick, and be indeed the pastor of his flock.

Even admitting the existence of a married clergy, it is not necessary that it form an hereditary caste. The caste once abolished, nothing would prevent the daughters of curés marrying decent farmers, the sons learning a business and settling in the village. Here, at one blow, is a riddance of many expenses.

These are reforms to be proposed. Meantime, is it true that the parish clergy are so miserable? As is easily understood, the revenues of the clergy in the towns, and especially in the large towns, are much more considerable than in the country. At Petersburg they are greater than in the provinces.

Let us begin, then, by seeing if the curés of the principal parishes of the capital are in distress. Here is the information furnished by our author, to whom the subject seems very familiar:

The curés of Petersburg have not to trouble

themselves about their dwelling: apartments
are gratuitously provided for them, such as
could not be rented for less than 160*l.*, 240*l.*,
or 320*l.* per ann. The furniture is from the
first shops of Petersburg. Rich carpets cover
the floors of the drawing-room, study, and
chamber; the windows display fine hangings;
the walls, valuable pictures. Footmen in livery
are not rarely seen in the anteroom. The din-
ners given by these curés are highly appre-
ciated by the most delicate epicures. Occa-
sionally their *salons* are open for a soirée or a
ball; ordinarily it is on the occasion of a wed-
ding, or the birthday of the curé, or on the
patron saint's day. The apartments are then
magnificently lighted up, the toilettes of the
ladies dazzling; the dancing is to the music
of an orchestra of from seven to ten musicians.
At supper, the table is spread with delicacies,
and champagne flows in streams. A Petersburg curé recently deceased loved to relate,
that at his daughter's nuptials champagne was
drunk to the value of 300 roubles (48*l.*).

In the provinces they are more modest;
yet the towns try to imitate the capital. The
rooms of the curé are here less splendid; the
furniture, however, is chiefly of walnut and
mahogany, and includes large mirrors, carpets,
and often a piano. The curé's daughters are

dressed by the milliner of the place; you will always see them attired with elegance; they do not discard crinoline, and never go out without a parasol. The curé himself wears cloth, silk, and sometimes velvet; and our anonymous friend jovially informs us that the reverend gentleman gives at his parsonage soirées and balls, at the latter of which the daughters of priests dance with the young men of the seminaries, to the great scandal of the superiors of these institutions. Let us carefully recollect this word, which escapes our author in spite of himself; it is to the credit of the seminaries, and consoles us by permitting us to hope that this clergy is not completely lost.

The country curés are evidently far from leading such a life as the urban. Yet it appears that for the last twenty years it has not been rare, even in the villages, to see the wives and daughters of priests display over their crinolines no longer merely modest dresses of cotton, but of wool and silk. They wear mantles, burnous, and small Garibaldi hats. It is very true that they sometimes divest themselves of this attire to labour in the fields. It is also true that their table-fare is very modest; they do not eat meat every day, even on the days when they are not required to abstain. In many Russian villages this is a real necessity, and our author strives in vain to move our pity for the fate of these poor curés. From this description it evidently results, that if they are unfortunate, it is because they compare themselves to their brethren of the large towns, especially to those of Petersburg. If, on the contrary, they would compare themselves to the peasants among whom they live, they would be obliged to confess that they were better lodged, better clothed, and better nourished than their flocks. Our author says that it is painful to be bareheaded when one accompanies a dead body to the cemetery, or follows a procession, and that it is very disagreeable to confess rude and ignorant people. These complaints give us the measure of importance to be attached to them. Besides, who, then, must be held responsible for the ignorance of the peasants? Who would be bound to instruct them, if not the curé? Let us remark, again, that, in spite of the very severe laws which oblige every Russian to confess every year, it is rare that one has to hear more than half the persons of an age to fulfil this Easter duty. Too often it is only the fourth part, sometimes even the tenth. As to confessing more than once a year, it is a fact almost unheard of, especially in the country. The anonymous writer farther adds: ' The

curés are steeped in humiliation, and exposed
to incessant and vexatious exactions on the
part of the diocesan authorities.' This is another question, and a new proof that, even to
better the material condition of the clergy, it
is not sufficient to add to their revenues.

We saw just now that the clergy of a Russian parish regularly consist of a priest, a deacon, and two clerks. Two-thirds of the parishes
have no deacons; they do without them very
well. The others would do without them in
like manner. The presence of the deacon gives
to the services more solemnity and splendour,
an advantage the importance of which I appre-
ciate; but I put in view the 400,000*l.* which
these 12,444 deacons cost Russia, without
speaking of the thousands of hectares which
are allotted them. It seems to me that they
are rather dear. Still, if these 12,444 fathers
of families, their wives and their children, were
happy! But it is not so. By the very force of
things, the existence of the deacon is a painful one. His situation is false, subordinate;
he has before him no future; his wants are
almost the same as the priest's, while he has
only the half of the latter's resources. The
character with which he is clothed forbids him
the exercise of many professions, without open-
ing to him access to the laborious practical

functions of the ministry. His office ended, the Church has no farther need of him. To recite every Sunday an indefinite number of *ektenias** is not enough to fill up the life of a man. In the Catholic Church, the Mass is sung with deacon and subdeacon. The deacon is also employed in solemn offices; but, instead of maintaining a deacon who could render no other services, they prefer to have a second priest, who aids the first in all the functions of the holy ministry, who replaces him at need, and who at the altar acts as deacon whenever it is necessary. I do not see why something like this should not be done in the Russian Church. It is true that the deacon could fill the office of schoolmaster; but, on looking closer into the matter, one will soon be convinced that the more practicable thing is the suppression of deacons in the parishes.

Beside the 12,444 deacons, the Russian Church still possesses 63,421 clerks, who discharge the duties of readers, chanters, sacristans, beadles, and ringers.† They form part of

---

* *Ektenia*, from ἐκτενὴς, *extended*, signifies an *enlarged* prayer. It consists of short petitions, each followed by the response from singers and people of 'Lord, have mercy,' or 'Lord, hear us,' or 'Grant us, Lord,' as in the Litany of the English Episcopal Church. (*Trans.*)

† All these inferior clerical degrees are comprised under the generic Russian term *prichetniki* (причетники), from причетъ, clergy, retinue.

the clergy, take part of the perquisites, and, farther, are enrolled in the caste. As the figures show, there are ordinarily two clerks to a parish. Their maintenance costs 600,000*l.*, or 9*l.* 10*s.* per head. Each has, besides, four hectares to cultivate, and creates resources from cows, pigs, poultry, kitchen-garden, &c. Sometimes they follow a trade, as that of a glazier, bookbinder, &c.

The Eastern Liturgy is extremely long, and if the reader read in an intelligible manner, the whole day would be passed in church. Respect for ancient tradition permits of no retrenchment; on the other hand, it is not wished that the Mass should last more than an hour, and the other offices in proportion. To accomplish this, the reader reads with such a volubility, that it is impossible to understand anything; and sometimes, in order to proceed still faster, two read at the same time different parts.* And then they come and reproach us

---

* One hundred and fifty years ago, Peter the Great, in his *Spiritual Regulation*, remarked that, 'The very clerics, by discharging their duties in a perfunctory manner, have originated and established a custom of *double praying* and *singing*, and even of giving *several* readings and chantings at the same time; so that the morning and evening prayers, divided into sections, are performed by several persons concurrently. And whereas this innovation, the fruit of sloth, is vicious and utterly opposed to God's appointment, such a mode of discharging the divine offices is to be entirely abandoned.' *Spir. Reg.* part ii. Common Affairs, ix. (*Trans.*)

with celebrating the Mass in Latin, in a language not understood by the vulgar!

The first reform in this matter would be to abridge the offices, to retain only that which can be read and sung with edification. One clerk alone would then suffice, and he not necessarily selected from the children of ecclesiastics. Besides, I see no reason why a layman of good life and manners should not be taken to do the work of a clerk. He might have a trade; he might be a shoemaker, or a tailor, no matter what. Except on holidays and Sundays, he would have little to do at church. He would not take his share of the perquisites, nor of the lands of the church; but he would receive a fixed salary. When the curé became dissatisfied with him, he would discharge him and take another. Let us here remark that the 63,000 families of these clerks form the great majority of the caste, and that it is of great concern to subject them to the jurisdiction of the common law. These reforms once made, there would probably be no inconvenience in the parish clerk becoming at the same time the village schoolmaster. It would, however, be necessary to clearly lay down that there is no connection between these two employments.

It now remains for us to say a few words on

the more or less voluntary contributions of the parishioners, and the mode of collecting them.

We first notice a species of tithe paid in kind. Towards the Feast of St. Peter each house gives from three to five eggs, and a little milk, with which cheese and butter are made. In autumn, after the gathering of the crops, each house gives a certain quantity of wheat. When a child is born, the priest repairs to the house of the mother, recites over her a few prayers, and gives a name to the new-born babe. This service brings him a loaf, with 2*d*. or 4*d*.; the baptism from 4*d*. to 1*s*. more. Six weeks after, new prayers bring him a dozen eggs. At betrothals the priest receives a loaf, some brandy, sometimes a goose or a sucking-pig. Marriage costs from 8 to 16 francs (6*s*. 8*d*. to 13*s*. 4*d*.); interment, from 3*s*. 4*d*. to 6*s*. 8*d*. The fee for Masses for the dead is from 1*s*. 2*d*. to 2*s*. 8*d*.; the prayers recited for the dead (an oft-repeated practice) bring each time from 2*d*. to 4*d*. Now there is a sort of *De profundis*, and now a *Memento*. When these prayers are read at the cemetery, which takes place every year on certain days, the peasant gives the priest some rice, a cake, or some pastry. Frequently the peasants have a *Te Deum* chanted as a thanksgiving for some favour received, or a supplication for some

new gifts from God, or simply on the occasion of their birth- or name-days, or in some
other circumstance. Each time they give the
priest from 4d. to 8d. It is a custom in Russia
that the penitent, on receiving absolution, gives
money to the confessor. In towns this sum
frequently rises to 4s., 8s., and 16s., sometimes to much more. In the villages the peasant offers only 4 centimes (a kopec, about
½d.); but on receiving the communion, he is
obliged to renew his offering several times: for
prayers before communion, at the moment of
communion, after communion, and for having
his name enrolled, &c. During the Masses
collections are made, and a portion of the sum
assigned to the clergy. It even sometimes
happens that the priest, arrayed in his sacerdotal ornaments, traverses the whole church,
the censer in one hand, and the other open to
receive the offerings of the parishioners.

Another source of revenue are the prayers
chanted at home in every house in the parish.
This takes place at Easter, at Christmas, at
the Epiphany, at the beginning and end of
Lent, and on the patron saint's day, which
is repeated in certain places twice or thrice
a year. Our author cites one of his friends,
who assured him that the clergy of his parish,
in St. Petersburg, in this way presented them-

selves to him as many as twenty-seven times; but he regards this case as an exaggeration or an exception. Generally, they come, says he, no more than fifteen times. At each visit the master of the house must give something. At Petersburg, and in the towns, these prayers bring sufficiently large amounts; in the villages they give, according to the importance of the day, 2*d.*, 4*d.*, 10*d.*, 1*s.* 8*d.*, or 2*s.* 6*d.*; which, on the average, amounts to 7*s.* 6*d.* or 8*s.* per year per house. We have no means of verifying these figures, and are obliged to give them just as we find them in the anonymous writer, who, as we have said, seems perfectly well informed, and more inclined to lessen than to exaggerate the resources of the White clergy. Following him, the voluntary contributions should be estimated at one rouble, or 3*s.* 4*d.* per head, reckoning only the male population. This makes many shillings per family. We must, however, include in the reckoning baptisms, marriages, interments, and in general everything for which the peasant pays to the clergy.

Sometimes it happens that the peasant cannot or will not give what the priest asks. Hence arise angry disputes. One priest—so runs the story—unable to overcome the obstinacy of a peasant refusing to pay for the

prayers read in his house, declared to him that
he would reverse them. He had just before
chanted ' *Benedictus Deus noster;*' he now
intoned ' NON *Benedictus*, NON *Deus*, NON *noster;*' thus intercalating a *non* after every word.
The affrighted peasant, the chronicle says,
instantly complied.* Often enough, too, in
spite of all the prohibitions of the Synod, the
wives and children of the priests, deacon, and
clerks accompany their husbands and fathers,
and stretch out *their* hands also. The worst
of all this is, that the Russian peasant, while
long disputing merely about a few centimes,
will think himself insulted unless the priest
accept a glass of brandy. And when the cir-
cuit of all the houses in the village has to be
made, though he stay only a few minutes in
each, this last gift is not without its inconveniences.

It must, then, be recognised, that if the
revenues of the clergy are far from being as
insufficient as is pretended, the mode of collecting them admits of improvement. A reform is necessary, but it will be difficult. On
the one hand, the clergy will not renounce

---

* The superstitions pervading a great part of the Russian people might form matter for a volume, and indeed we have been
told that a dictionary of Russian superstitions was published in
Russia in 1782. To check their influence and growth, several
articles are inserted in the Russian Code of Law. (*Trans.*)

this source of revenue; on the other, it is impossible to convert these voluntary contributions into compulsory imposts. A system of tariffs might perhaps be introduced, at the same time making the people understand that by this regulation no new charges were imposed, but only a change made in the mode of collection.

In completing this picture of the situation of the parish clergy in the Russian Church, and of the reforms which it imperatively demands, it is impossible for me to pass by in silence a reflection which here presents itself. I by no means desire to become the champion of the Protestant clergy. As to the Catholic clergy, I know very well that, notwithstanding the grace attached to the sacerdotal character, the infirmity of human nature is sometimes revealed by many miseries. In the Catholic clergy there can exist abuses and disorders: these have been, and still are, more or less, according to different countries. Without going far for examples, the joy we feel from the marvellous transformation wrought under our eyes in the German clergy must not make us forget the tears wrung from us 50 or 30 years ago. I admit it; but in spite of that, I do not believe that there is in the Catholic Church, or even in the Protestant churches, a clergy fallen so low

as the Russian, and which answers so little to
what we might justly expect it to be.' This
unhappy clergy appears to have reached the
point of self-persuasion that all its duties are
fulfilled in chanting the offices. As to making
Jesus Christ known and loved, or pointing out
to souls the way to tread in His steps, it does
not even dream of such a thing. The salvation of souls redeemed by Jesus Christ at the
price of His own blood concerns it not; its
thought goes not beyond a few formalities understood after a Jewish fashion.

Now, let us very loudly assert it, the fault
is not in the individuals. I am convinced that
the clergy counts in its ranks well-disposed
men, good men, who profoundly sigh over the
situation made for them. Where, then, must
we look for the root of the evil? In the vicious
organisation of the clergy; in this obligation
of marriage imposed on all the aspirants to
the priesthood—an obligation unknown to the
canonical law of the East, and which has resulted in making the clergy an hereditary caste.
There are yet other causes, doubtless, of which
we shall have occasion to speak; but here we
would above all call attention to this grave
abuse, so fertile of disastrous consequences.

May these few pages impress on those who
can apply a remedy to the evil, how urgent it

is to enter on the path of reform; how necessary to prevent the White clergy in Russia being any longer an hereditary caste; and finally, how desirable it is to create, by the side of the married and the Black, a clergy secular and celibate.

In view of these enormous abuses, we can only desire the adoption of the reforms which we have just sketched; but a reflection confronts us. Who will execute these reforms? The Russian Church, had it the will, has not the necessary authority to cause their adoption. Will the government? It would evidently transgress the limits of its sphere and trespass on the rights of the Church. This shows the radically false situation in which the Russian Church is placed, and proves to us that it is outside herself and outside the government that she can alone find a remedy for the evils which ruin her. We reserve to ourselves to examine hereafter this aspect of the question.

CHAPTER II.

WE read in the Gospel that one day a young man accosted our Lord, and asked Him what he must do to have eternal life. 'Keep the commandments,' replied the divine Saviour. In that magnificent discourse addressed to His Apostles after the Last Supper, our Lord said unto them, 'If ye love Me, keep my commandments;' 'He who keepeth my commandments, he it is that loveth Me.' (John xiv. 21, 23.) And at the moment of His ascension, He pronounced these solemn words: 'Go, instruct all nations, teaching them whatsoever I have commanded you.' (Matt. xxviii. 18, 20.)

'Keep the commandments;' here is the law, here is that which is rigorously necessary to insure one's salvation. But, besides the commandments, the divine Legislator has given men counsels: 'If thou wilt be perfect,' said He to the young man who questioned Him, 'sell all that thou hast, and give to the poor, and come, follow Me.' (Matt. xix. 21.)

This is not a commandment, a law binding on all Christians; it is counsel given by our Lord, a means of attaining the perfect life.

Because the counsel is not addressed to every one, it is not, therefore, to be concluded that it is addressed to no one; because it is not obligatory, it does not follow that none ought to follow it.

Always, everywhere, there have been, there are, there will be souls whom God calls in the way of His counsels; always, everywhere, there are, there have been, there will be souls who will respond to this call, and who will feel such response to be for them a necessity. Such souls very quickly learn that, to conform to the counsels of the Saviour, they must make them their rule of life. Hence the religious life, with its vows of poverty, chastity, and obedience.

The foundation of this kind of life is poverty, the renunciation of all personal property. The Utopian follies of Communism have shown us that a society could not be based on the renunciation of personal property without the concurrent renunciation of marriage and family: hence the vow of chastity. Lastly, every society necessarily supposes in its bosom an authority to which its members must submit: hence the vow of obedience. We here indicate only in their general features the funda-

mental bases of the religious life. Before
formulating counsels, our Lord says, 'If ye
will be perfect.' Poverty, chastity, obedience,
are, then, means of attaining to perfection, root-
ing out the three principal sources of our mis-
takes and our falls: the love of wealth, the
love of sensual pleasure, and pride.

Our Lord, when bidding the young man in
the Gospel 'sell that thou hast,' adds, 'come,
and follow Me.' To follow Jesus Christ is to
tread in His steps, to imitate the examples
He has given us. By the vows of poverty,
chastity, and obedience, the religious man imi-
tates Jesus Christ, treads in His steps. Our
Saviour went about doing good. He prayed,
suffered, preached, instructed the ignorant, permitted little children to approach Him, suc-
coured the miserable. The religious endeavour
to imitate Him. None of them can do all at
once. Some give themselves to the contemplative life, some to the active, some unite
both. Some propose to employ themselves in
works of spiritual mercy, others in those of
temporal: hence the variety of orders and institutions.

None of these orders is indispensable to the
Church; yet there would be some loss to the
fulness of church life and action, if the *religious*
element in her bosom were to be suppressed.

Besides, what earthly authority has the right to say, 'Henceforth no one shall follow the counsel of Jesus Christ'?

If thus of the Church in general, still less of the Oriental Church can the idea be entertained of the destruction of the religious state, where, by virtue of a discipline in force for centuries, it is almost uniquely among the religious that celibate priests are found, and the members of the Episcopate can be recruited. By this double title, the religious in the East exercise a greater influence than elsewhere, and hold there a position of more consideration.

All this perfectly applies to the Russian Church. Let us farther add, that from all time the monks have been singularly popular in Russia. Every page of history bears witness of it, and indeed this popularity must have become deeply rooted, since it has survived the decadence of monasteries. The married priest, or, to employ the word in common use, the *pope*, is not popular; the pope's wife and children are still less so. Notwithstanding all, the monk retains the favour of the faithful. This popularity is even to-day, weakened though it be, his only force, his only power.

The anonymous author of the book on *The White and Black Clergy*, blinded by his prejudices, has understood nothing of all this. He seriously quotes *Le Juif errant* (*Wandering Jew*), *Le Maudit* (*The Accursed*), and other works of the same kind. After this, is it astonishing that he should understand nothing of the religious life ? He sees in the Russian monasteries only two things—riches and abuses. The riches he exaggerates, and concludes on the necessity of confiscating them ; the abuses he describes, not for the purpose of reform, but to provoke the suppression of the religious orders.

A few words on the riches. We must first of all make a distinction between the treasures of the churches and the wealth of the monasteries. In the churches, in the sacristies are collected chalices, censers, chandeliers, embroidered copes and chasubles, fine pearls, images covered with gold and silver plates adorned with turquoises, rubies, emeralds, and diamonds. I readily recognise that all this wealth can represent a considerable amount ; but the monks are guardians of it rather than proprietors : they can take away no part to their personal use ; in a word, they are none the richer for it.

I know well that it is easy to find economists who, at sight of this unproductive capital, would advise a different use of it. I would that they first used this reasoning to all the ladies wearing diamonds. I very much doubt *their* finding it conclusive.

A Catholic Bishop of the United States met one day at Rome, in front of St. Peter's, a citizen of the great transatlantic republic. The latter, filled with admiration at sight of the immense basilica, asked the prelate if it would not be possible to erect such an edifice in America. 'Why not?' replied the Bishop, who was unwilling to wound his national pride. 'And do you think that one would realise interest from the capital?' Fancy St. Peter's at Rome belonging to a company paying a dividend to the shareholders!

When Mary Magdalene poured on the feet of the Saviour a costly perfume, having broken the alabaster box which contained it, those present, seeing her prodigality, murmured against her; but the divine Saviour defended her. And so with the gold and silver, the fine pearls and precious stones employed in the adorning of the churches. There is no investment of money here; but a sensible witness of the faith of populations, who give of their abundance to increase the splendour of worship and the magnificence of the temples of the God they adore.

It is true there are circumstances when the clergy can and ought to sacrifice even the

consecrated cups in order to relieve the necessities of the suffering members of Jesus Christ;
but from this it cannot be inferred that we
may confiscate these treasures. What finance
minister would dare to propose for signature
to the Emperor of Russia a measure, before
which Peter I. and Catherine II. checked themselves, and on which Biren himself was unable
to resolve?

Let us then leave on one side the treasures
laid up in the churches and sacristies of the
monasteries, and speak of the revenues and
properties of the monks. All this wealth was
confiscated more than a hundred years ago by
Catherine II. The history of this confiscation
is curious. It has been written with greater
care than clearness by M. Vladimir Milutin,
whose work was published from 1859 to 1861,
in the Memoirs of the Antiquarian Society of
Moscow.* We will make a few extracts from
this document.

In ancient times the clergy enjoyed great
immunities, which, without having ever been
sanctioned by general legislation, were the
result of special privileges and charters ac-

---

* Чтенія въ Императорскомъ Обществѣ Исторіи и Древностей рос-
сійскихъ при Московскомъ Университетѣ.–Повременное изданіе. Москва,
бъ Универс. Типогр. 8vo. Milutin's work bears the title of О нед-
вижимымъ немуществахъ духовенства въ россіи–Излеѣдованіе Владим.
Милютина, in the No. of Oct.-Dec. 1859, et seq.

corded to each monastery. These privileges
display great variety. Generally the goods
of the clergy were exempt from taxes; their
administration exclusively belonged to the
monasteries or to the bishops; justice was ad-
ministered therein, not by the representatives
of the prince, but by those of the ecclesiastical
authority: so that the ecclesiastical domains
formed almost independent states. All the
public powers, including the Khans of the
Golden Horde,'* contributed to create this
state of things. Reaction began to show itself
in the sixteenth century, under the last princes
of the house of Ruric. Against the excessive
growth of the wealth of the clergy they took
measures which were not applied in all their
rigour.

When one thinks of the circumstances
which brought about and accompanied the accession of the Romanoffs to the throne, one is
led to conclude that this dynasty ought to
have testified to the clergy the liveliest grati-
tude and the most unbounded confidence. It
has been quite otherwise. The young Michel

---

* A son of the Mongol Genghis Khan became in 1223 the first
governor of the province lying between the Dnieper and the Ural
(according to some authors, between the Don and the Volga),
and in a part of Turkestan. The horde, or tribe, to which he
belonged, he named the 'Golden Horde,' which designation was
later given to that whole region. (*Trans.*)

could not, during the life of the patriarch his father, attack ecclesiastical privileges; but the tsar Alexis determined on a radical measure respecting the wealth of the clergy. He established, under the name of *Monastyrski Prikaz* (chancery of the monasteries), a kind of tribunal charged to acquaint itself with all the proceedings relating to this wealth, and at the same time to administer it, to draw up the leases, and to levy the taxes. The bishops, the monasteries, the churches, preserved the properties of their domains, and received the revenues of them; the administration, the collection, and the accounting were withdrawn from them. As was easy to be foreseen, after this intervention of bureaucracy, their revenues considerably diminished. Moreover, they were subjected to a very troublesome control. The establishment of the *Monastyrski Prikaz* played a great part in the deposition of the patriarch Nicon. It is surprising that M. Vladimir Milutin says nothing about it.

Immediately after the death of the tsar Alexis, this tribunal was abolished. Peter I., a few years later, reëstablished it; and under different names, with slight modifications, it stood, almost without interruption, until the radical measure taken by Catherine.

Peter I. had fixed the taxes according to

the needs of each convent, and had taken care
to put them low enough. The sum fixed by
Peter was first levied on the revenues of each
convent, and handed to the monks; the sur-
plus was applied as the *well-being of the Church
and country demanded!* Sometimes the same
motives engaged the sovereign to dispose, not
only of the revenues, but also of the properties themselves. Thus vast ecclesiastical domains were granted to Menchikoff. Peter had
thought of giving to the monasteries pension-
ers—the invalids of his army, and convicts who
were old and infirm, maimed or mad. The invalids, convicts, and monks received the same
rations. The reforming tsar complained of the
ignorance of the monks; probably for this it
was that he harshly forbade them to have in
their cells pens, ink, and paper. Moreover,
none could be admitted to the religious profession without an imperial ukase.

When the dynasty of Romanoff became
extinct in the person of Elizabeth, the crown
passed to the dynasty of Holstein Gottorp.
Peter III. had nothing to do but renew and
confirm the acts of the Romanoffs in order to
consummate the confiscation of ecclesiastical
property. The measures which he prescribed
excited no less the lively discontent of the
clergy; and it was one of the grievances

brought against him at the revolution which deprived him of both throne and life. Scarcely had Catherine II. deemed her authority sufficiently established than she took up the project of Peter III., and by her ukase of Feb. 26th, 1764, seized on all the ecclesiastical lands.

There was no resistance except on the part of Arsenius Matseievich, Archbishop of Rostoff, who was degraded in 1764, and, confined in a narrow prison at Revel as a *vral* (or dotard), died there in 1772.

We note farther, that in a ukase relating to the same subject, and dated Aug. 12th, 1762 (the revolution which had put Catherine II. on the throne had taken place June 28th of the same year, and Peter III. died July 6th), the tsarina said she received from God, as did all monarchs, the chief authority in the Church.

Upon the vast domains confiscated in 1764 there was a population of 910,866 peasants, without reckoning women.* They were instantly taxed 1 rouble 50 kopecs (5s.) per head, and the first year brought to the crown 1,366,229 roubles, or 227,705l. On this sum the state levied 403,712 roubles (67,285l.) for allowances to the clergy, and thus profited by

---

* Two-thirds belonged to the monasteries, one-third to the bishops, to the cathedrals, &c.

160,420*l.* Soon after, it was felt necessary to
increase the tax on the rents of the peasantry.
In 1772 it was 2 roubles 70 kopecs (9*s.*), and
in 1783 3 roubles 70 kopecs (12*s.* 4*d.*). In
proportion as the charges on the peasants became heavier, the crown revenues became more
considerable.   In 1783 the confiscated wealth
brought 3,370,000 roubles, or 541,666*l.* 13*s.* 4*d.*
We know not to what sum the state receipts ac-
cruing from this head can now amount.   Let
us say only that the allowances to the orthodox
clergy figure, in the budget for 1865, for a
sum of 5,806,210 roubles, or 967,701*l.* 13*s.* 4*d.*
We may hence conclude that the confiscation
of 1764 has not enriched the treasury, but has
placed it face to face with the growing complaints and exigences of the clergy.

But all this concerns the past: the question is, how much the revenues of the convents
now amount to.   Our anonymous author does
not give us the exact figure, which, besides,
is not known.   An approximate idea can, however, be obtained by passing in review the
different sources from which they are drawn.
These are state aid, immovables, as fisheries,
mills, meadows, forests, arable lands, &c.   All
other means of income can be comprised under
the term alms.   Let us examine in detail these
different resources.

The ukase of February 26th, 1764, was not confined to the confiscation of the goods of the clergy; it suppressed the greater part of the convents. Those which were preserved were divided into two categories: the convents state-aided, and those which were not.

The first category comprehends monasteries of the first, second, and third classes. Among the first-class convents are seven more important than the rest, denominated *Stauropegia*. Above and beyond these three classes are four great *Laures:* that of the *crypts* at Kieff; that of St. Sergius, or of the Trinity, in the environs of Moscow; that of St. Alexander Nevsky, at St. Petersburg; and, finally, that of Potchayeff, in Volhynia, taken from the United Greeks in 1833.

The state-aided monasteries receive an annual allowance which may be regarded as a sort of indemnity for the confiscated wealth; but it is plain that this allowance is far from representing the value of the property taken. In a monastery of the first class this aid is thus divided:

	R.	K.
The archimandrite	500	0
„ vicar	50	0
„ treasurer	25	0
Eight priests, at 13 roubles . .	104	0
Four deacons, „ „ . .	52	0

	R.	K.
Two guardians, at 10 roubles . . .	20	0
A baker, a housekeeper, and eight monks, at 9 roubles	99	0
Five overseers of infirmary, at 8 roubles .	40	0
Lay employés: writer at 19 roubles, and twenty-four servants at 9 roubles; supplementary, 55 roubles . . .	290	0
Maintenance and repair of church . .	400	0
Keep for horses	62	50
Wood-fuel	150	0
Hospitality	100	0
Beer and brandy	125	0
Total	2017	50

= £336 5s.

A monastery of the second class receives 1611 roubles 90 k. (268l. 14s.); a monastery of the third class, 670 roubles 30 k. (111l. 14s. 4d.)*

An official report of Count Protassoff for 1850 gives us the number of the monasteries of each class, which enables us to estimate the amount of the aid. Thus we shall have

			R.	K.
39 convents of 1st class .	.	.	78,682	50
65 ,, 2d ,, .	.	.	104,733	50
113 ,, 3d ,, .	.	.	75,743	90
Total .	.	.	.	259,199	90

= £43,200.

It is true that in 1842, in the western pro-

---

* Silbernagl, *Verfassung und gegenwärtiger Bestand sämmtlicher Kirchen des Orients* (Landshut, 1865), pp. 133, 134.

vinces, the allowances were more considerable. Here are the figures:

Convents, 1st class, 3185 R. = £509 12s.
    ,,   2d ,, 2220 R. = 355 4s.
    ,,   3d ,, 1540 R. = 246 8s.

which makes, supposing in a convent of first-class 30 monks, more than 400 francs per head. It was very necessary to pay for the apostasy of the United-Greek monks turned orthodox in 1839.

We have in the first chap. (p. 33) spoken of the perpetual endowments, invested in state funds at 4 per cent, assigned to the clergy, with an obligation to pray for the departed. This sum amounted to 64,000,000 roubles (10,240,000l.); giving a revenue of 2,560,000 roubles, or of 426,666l. 13s. 4d. We know not what share of this revenue goes to the regular clergy. It ought to receive at least the half of it.

After the confiscation of 1764, the state again allowed another kind of indemnity to the convents. They had lost their serfs; in order to replace them the state sent into each of the state-aided monasteries a certain number of peasants, for indoor service. They were obliged to live there twenty-five years, after which they returned to their villages, and were replaced by others. These servants were gratuitously furnished by the state, to the number of twelve for convents of the third class, seventeen for those of the second class, and for the rest in proportion. At the emancipation of the serfs in 1861 the government rightly judged that it was time to put an end to an order of things which too much recalled the *corvée*, and the convents have since then received as indemnity a sum of 307,850 silver roubles (51,308*l.*). By adding, then, the two state subsidies together, we shall have for the monasteries for men,

	R.	K.
	259,199	90
	307,850	0
Total . .	567,049	90 = £94,508

which does not appear exorbitant, if it is considered that the maintenance of the orthodox clergy figures in the budget of 1865 for the sum of 5,806,210 silver roubles (967,701*l.*). Let us now pass to the immovables.

After the ukase of 1764 the Russian monasteries could no longer possess lands inhabited by peasants bound to the soil; but they retained fisheries, mills, meadows, woods, arable lands, and they have the right to acquire them. The state itself gave them, and continues to give them from time to time, properties of this

F

kind. On December 18th, 1797, the Emperor
Paul published a ukase which accords thirty
hectares of land to all the convents subsidised
or not. During twenty years, from 1842 to
1861, 168 convents received 16,879 hectares;
which on an average gives 100 hectares per
convent. In 1858, 1240 hectares of wood were
allotted to the Laure of St. Sergius, Moscow.
The twenty-four convents of the province of
Novgorod possess 9641 hectares. In 1861 the
convent of Saroff, in the government of Tam-
boff, felled 6000 hectares of wood.

The mere gum gathered from the resinous
trees of the forests belonging to this convent
has been sold for 1920*l.* From all this we
must conclude that, spite of the confiscation of
1764, the Russian monasteries still possess immovables of sufficiently great value.

But the bulk of the revenue of these houses
comes from another source. The Russians
freely give to the convents, and the generosity
of the Russian people is every moment soli-
cited by inventions the most varied and in-
genious. The rich and great are fond of being
buried within the precincts of the monasteries;
and these places are sold at very high prices.
The interments, the prayers requested to be
offered at the tombs of relatives, bring to the
monks very handsome sums. Begging Bro-

thers traverse all Russia gathering alms. In the densest thoroughfares, in large towns, on roads, are sometimes seen chapels, or oratories, in which no Mass is said, but some venerated image stands exposed. These chapels are much frequented by the Russian people, and each visitor there purchases a wax-taper, or drops some money into the box. The images reputed miraculous, as also the relics of the saints, are ordinarily in the churches of the convents, where they attract enormous crowds, and no one comes empty-handed. Some years ago the Synod canonised a bishop named Tychon. The solemn transfer of his relics, which is equivalent to the ceremony of canonisation, drew together 250,000 persons. It is asserted that the *laure* of St. Sergius receives every year a million of pilgrims. The celebrated image of our Lady of Iberia, which is exposed in a chapel built against the walls of the Kremlin at Moscow, belongs to the convent of Pererva. It is estimated that the receipts of this chapel in 1843 amounted to 16,000*l.*

According to the *Golos** (1865, No. 283), the single *laure* of St. Sergius has a revenue of at least two millions. That of the *Crypts* at Kieff is also extremely rich. Our anonymous author accumulates a great number of quota-

* Голосъ (Petersburg daily newspaper).

tions and figures, in order to show with what skill, and often with what astuteness, the religious spirit and credulity of the Russian people are worked upon by the monks. We are inclined to think that in these estimates there is some exaggeration; but it is difficult to refuse all credence to what our author relates.

What use is made of all these riches? Are they employed in missions, in the relief of the poor, in founding hospitals, schools, colleges, libraries? We can boldly reply, that but a very small part of the revenue of the convents has this destination. It is a notorious fact, that a portion of the alms is misappropriated by the very persons who gather them. Then in the monasteries where the community-life (*la vie commune*) is not established—and these are by far the more numerous—a third of the revenues forms the share of the superior, who lives in luxury, and very often enriches his family. According to the *Voice* (*Golos*), 1865, No. 283, the revenues of the superiors of convents should be estimated as follows:

In the Convents of the

3d class, 1,000 to 5,000 R. silver.	= £160 to £800
2d ,, 5,000 ,, 10,000 ,,	= 800 ,, 1600
1st ,, 10,000 ,, 30,000 ,,	= 1600 ,, 4800

In the Laures—

40,000 to 60,000 R. silver. = £6400 to £9600

Our author proposes to the government to re-
sume and complete the measure taken in 1764,
that is to say, to confiscate once more the convent property. This would be in our eyes
an injustice, and a serious attack on the rights
of property. We farther think, that in all
these figures there is much fancy. In taking
the average of the expense of maintaining the
monks, their novices, and their aspirants, at
100 roubles (say 16*l*. 0*s*. 0*d*.) per year per
head, we take a very modest valuation, and
do not allow the means of living in luxury.
However, if you take into account the 10,000
monks, novices, and aspirants, who live in the
Russian convents, you will at once arrive at
the very respectable figure of 1,000,000 roubles, or 160,000*l*. At first this appears considerable; but divided by 10,000, it is a very
small matter. Let us even admit that the
sum be doubled, what men among those who
loudest inveigh against the riches of the
convents would consent to live on 32*l*. per
annum?

We do not think the convents to be so rich
as our anonymous author would wish to persuade us; but suppose them to be so, 'tis not
there that the evil lies. If the community-life
were everywhere introduced, if the superiors
were subjected thereto as the others, if they

could misappropriate nothing of the revenues for themselves or for their relations, it would not be difficult to find a useful purpose for the resources of the religious houses. Yes, schools are doubtless wanted in Russia, hospitals, hospices, orphanages, asylums for the aged, and many other good things; but instead of suppressing the monks and confiscating their property, so act that they themselves may organise all these useful works. They can do it better and more economically than bureaucracy.* The right of property will be respected, and justice will suffer no hurt.

The real scandal consists not in the greater

---

* What, without bureaucracy, may be done for the poor is finely shown by a Catholic religious Order known as the 'Little Sisters of the Poor,' whose founder, the Abbé le Pailleur, still lives, and whose whole life and labour are devoted to the feeding and nurturing of aged poor of both sexes and of every denomination. The Order, numbering between 800 and 1000 sisters, has in different countries the management of more than 150 asylums, sheltering over 15,000 inmates. The sisters' resources are limited to the free-will offerings of the charitable, given in response to daily applications at private houses and the public markets. The gifts from private houses consist of broken victuals, stale but clean bread, &c. At the markets the sisters good-humouredly submit to various receptions, and shrewdly take advantage of them, as recently seen in Covent-garden, London. In reply to their appeal, a rough market-gardener ironically bade them 'take that there sack of potatoes,' and was astounded to see the sturdier of the two eagerly shoulder the sack, and bear it off amid the laughter of the bystanders. It would be to the credit of the railway companies if these carers for the poor were permitted to travel free. (*Trans.*)

or less revenue that the convents can have,
but in the bad use made of it, and above all,
in the fact that this money serves to enrich
the superiors. Here is the evil to be uprooted.
Now Russian legislation, far from opposing,
encourages it.

What the anonymous author of the book on
the White and Black clergy, and the men who
have inspired him, wish, is simply to despoil
the celibate clergy of the alms received from
the people, in order to aid the toilet-expenses
of the wives and daughters of the married
priests. Let them at least have the courage to
say so.

Before speaking of abuses, let us glance at
the situation of the monasteries in Russia.

All are reputed to live under the rule of
St. Basil. They are not so united among themselves as to form one or several congregations.
Formerly it was not so. There were large
monasteries, to which were affiliated a greater
or less number of other convents, under the
guardianship and jurisdiction of the central
abbey. The *laure* of St. Sergius had forty
houses in its dependence. These salutary bonds
made the strength of the monastic Order; they
were a guarantee for the maintenance of discipline. In proportion as the hand of the State
has been extended over the Church, and has

taken away her independence, these bonds have been broken: the monasteries have been isolated, and hence have resulted also their weakness and decay.

The action of the state has made itself felt in yet another fashion. Formerly the convents were very numerous. In 1762, without reckoning Little Russia and White Russia, there were still

$$\left.\begin{array}{l} 732 \text{ convents of men }\, . \\ 222 \qquad ,, \qquad \text{women} \end{array}\right\} = 954$$

The ukase of Catherine II., which confiscated the property of the clergy, enacted that there should be thenceforward only

$$\left.\begin{array}{l} 361 \text{ convents of men }\, . \\ 39 \qquad ,, \qquad \text{women} \end{array}\right\} = 400$$

This was the suppression of 554 convents. Little by little this rigour was obliged to be relaxed, and ever since the number of convents has been increasing.

We have been able to procure the following figures:

						Total.
1810	. . . .					452
1815	. .	387	convents of men,	91	of women,	478
1830	. .	408	,,	101	,,	509
1836	. .	410	,,	102	,,	512
1837	. .	412	,,	103	,,	515
1838	. .	435	,,	113	,,	548

							Total.
1849	.	.	462 convents of men,	123 of women,	585
1850	.	.	464	„	123	„	587
1860	.	.	614*	„	137	„	751

The following are the figures of the religious of both sexes, according to the same documents :†

							Total.
1815	.	.	4900 monks,	1696 nuns,	6596
1818	.	.	—	„	—	„	7000
1835	.	.	4396	„	3161	„	7557
1836	.	.	4432	„	2544	„	6976
1837	.	.	5703	„	2655	„	8358
1838	.	.	6724	„	2352	„	9076
1849	.	.	5105	„	2595	„	7700
1850	.	.	4978	„	2313	„	7291

These figures present strange anomalies. It must be kept in view that the monasteries of the United Greeks, incorporated in 1839, are reckoned as part of the Russian Church in 1838. This explains the sudden increase of 1000 monks in one year. Already in the pre-

---

* We offer no explanation how the convents for men rose in the ten years 1850-60 by 150.

† These documents are:

(*a*) Mgr. Filaret, Archbishop of Kharkoff, recently deceased at the see of Tchernigoff: Исторія русской Церкви. Tchern. 1862, period v. p. 130.

(*b*) Fath. Theiner, *L'Eglise schismatique Russe*, pp. 416, 417.

(*c*) The Official Reports of the Count Protassoff for 1850 and 1851.

(*d*) The anonymous author of the book on the *White and Black Clergy*, vol. i. pp. 166, 210.

ceding year there had been an inexplicable increase of 1200 monks. We may suppose that they were United Greeks taken from their own convents, and incorporated into the Russian convents. But these unjust acquisitions have not profited the Russian Church; twelve years afterward there remained nothing of this momentary increase.

Alas, if these monks could rise from their tombs, and describe the manœuvres, frauds, violences by which they were successfully made to appear in the report presented by Count Protassoff to the Emperor Nicholas; if they could tell us by what accidents they successively disappeared from these sad lists! Did Siberia receive them? Did death deliver them? We cannot tell. We see only that these figures suddenly swell, then melt away like an avalanche which is precipitated into the valley, and quickly disappears under the rays of the sun.

In the figures we have cited let us point to another anomaly. The male religious are almost thrice as numerous as the female. Another document gives us the number of persons of both sexes admitted to the religious profession from 1841 to 1857, during a space of sixteen years, the year 1848 being excluded:

$$\left.\begin{array}{ll}\text{Men} & 4147 \\ \text{Women} & 1569\end{array}\right\} = 5716$$

The proportion between the two sexes is still almost the same. But if we take into our calculation the novices of the two sexes, the male and female aspirants, in a word the whole population of the cloisters, we shall obtain different figures, as we shall easily see by the following table:

		Men		Women		Total.
1835	. .	5739 men,		6411 women,		12,150
1836	. .	5978	,,	9271	,,	15,249
1837	. .	7163	,,	6089	,,	13,252
1838	. .	8339	,,	6385	,,	14,724
1861	. .	10,527	,,	—	,,	—

Which gives the following proportion:

		Men.		Women.	
1835	. .	47 per cent,		53 per cent.	
1836	. .	48	,,	52	,,
1837	. .	54	,,	46	,,
1838	. .	56	,,	48	,,

That is to say, that the female population of the cloisters is very nearly equal to the male. It results, then, from the figures, that in the convents of women, the number of novices and postulants is much greater than that of the professed.

		Professed.		Novices.		Total.
1835	. .	3161	. .	3250	. .	6411
1836	. .	2544	. .	3727	. .	6271
1837	. .	2655	. .	3454	. .	6089
1838	. .	2322	. .	4033	. .	6385

	Professed.	Novices.	Total.
1849	. . 2595	. . 5825	. . 8420
1850	. . 2313	. . 6230*	. . 8543

We think we find the cause of this anomaly
in a ukase of Peter the Great, which forbids
admission to the religious profession to all women, unmarried or widows, under 40 years old.†
Hence it is that many young persons live in
a convent and share the life of the professed
whilst waiting to attain the age for professing.
This waiting is sometimes prolonged for twenty
years or more. After a delay longer or shorter
some make professions, others return to the
world, others still continue to live in the cloister
without taking the vows. It is not, after this,
astonishing that the number of those termed
novices and aspirants should be more considerable than that of the professed.

Finally, the table already laid before the
reader presents a third irregularity, for which
we have found no explanation. How happens
it that in 1836 the number of the professed falls
off all at once by 617, whilst that of the aspirants increases by 477 ? The next year, on the
contrary, the number of the professed increases
by 111, and that of the aspirants decreases by

---

* The number of the novices and postulants in the convents
state aided is given only for the years 1849 and 1850.

† Russian Code, ed. 1857, tom. ix. art. 250.

273; and the year after we see 333 less professed and 579 more aspirants.

1836	. .	Professed − 617,	aspirants	+ 477
1837	. .	,, + 111	,,	− 273
1838	. .	,, − 333	,,	+ 579

Is it not the violent reunion of the United
Greeks which is the cause of these strange fluc-
tuations?

We have seen that in taking into account
novices and aspirants of both sexes, the convents of men and those of women have almost
the same number of inmates. If we farther
examine these figures, we shall see that the
monks and nuns are not recruited from the
same classes. From 1841 to 1857, as we have
already remarked, 4147 men and 1569 women were admitted to the religious profession.
Let us see to what classes of society both belong.

We distinguish five different classes—the
clergy, nobility, urban population, rural population, and the military. Under the term clergy
figures the whole caste of which we have
hitherto spoken, viz. priests, deacons, clerics,
with their wives and children. By nobility we
mean, besides the nobles properly so called, all
government employés, including physicians,
professors, and in general all persons belong-

ing to the liberal professions, or who occupy a
post in the administration.

The urban population comprises merchants,
citizens, artisans, and all who are in Russia understood by the term *raznotchintzy*.* To the
rural population belong the peasants of every
category. Finally, under the name military we
take into account, with the soldiers, their wives
and children. These explanations being given,
here is the proportion in which the monks are
recruited from these different classes :

Clergy	. . . . .	2253	. .	54·3 per cent.
Urban population	. .	944	. .	22·3 „
Rural „	. .	684	. .	16·3 „
Military	. . . .	141	. .	3·4 „
Nobility	. . . .	125	. .	3·0 „

* разночницы, literally men of different categories (разно, *razno*
—чинъ, *tchin*). Tchin=ceremonial, order, rank.

By *tchin* is meant also the ladder of ranks introduced by Peter I., and which subordinated nobility of birth to that of service.
Here ancestors and parchments were made to count for nothing.
This civil institution was intended by Peter to weaken the old
nobility, and at first consisted of sixteen ranks, but afterwards
was reduced to fourteen. Of these, the first eight conferred hereditary nobility, with all the rights and privileges enjoyed by the
old ; to the ninth and tenth ranks only personal nobility was
awarded. Men of merit were by Peter introduced into any rank
he deemed proper ; but Paul I. ordained that the rise of all men
should be gradual, and taken strictly through all the steps of the
ladder successively. Recent municipal modifications have made
hereditary nobility more dependent on the Tsar's will, as also the
rights and privileges of that which is personal. See, for further
information, Schnitzler (J. H.), *L'Empire des Tsars au point actuel
de la Science*, Paris, 1866, tom. iii, seconde section, chap. 1, *La
société politique; état principal, constitution*, pp. 280-290. (*Trans.*)

For the nuns we have these figures:

Urban population . .	608	. .	38·8 per cent.
Rural „ . .	492	. .	31·0 „
Clergy	213	. .	13·0 „
Nobility	190	. .	12·0 „
Military	66	. .	4·0 „

Thus the majority of the monks belongs to the 'tribe of Levi,' whilst only one-eighth of the nuns comes from its ranks. The reason of this is very simple. We have seen that all the members of the Episcopate are taken from among the monks. Here is the motive which engages a good number of young men, at the close of their theological studies, to renounce marriage and adopt the religious habit. Nothing like this exists for women. There is, then, among the monks a whole category to which there is nothing analogous among the nuns.

The difference between the 4147 monks and the 1569 nuns is 2578; it answers very nearly to the figure 2253, which represents the number of monks proceeding from the sacerdotal caste.

We are presently to speak of this numerous category of monks, for whom the religious profession is a career far rather than a vocation. Merely observing now that these form the majority, we proceed to speak of the others.

The nobility, the administrative classes,

and the liberal professions annually give to the religious life, on an average, seven persons. This is little. The old soldiers furnish eight; 'tis scarcely worth while to note them. Forty-three vocations form the contingent of the rural population; fifty-nine that of the urban. The inhabitants of the country are eleven times more numerous than those of the towns, and it would besides seem that country life ought to dispose to the religious life rather than city tumult and corruption. Whence comes, then, this strange disproportion?

Russian legislation has put shackles on every religious vocation, which impede but little a rich merchant, but which a poor peasant succeeds only with the greatest difficulty in shaking off. This single fact ought to have great influence, and to explain, in part, why there are many more merchants than peasants in the convents. Farther, following our anonymous author, the convents exhibit but little eagerness to receive poor and ignorant peasants, who would be of no advantage to them, while they readily embrace merchants, who bring, besides their fortune, large experience in business and valuable connections with the commercial class. It is also an object of desire to have such men at the head of poor convents, which very soon prosper under their able management. They, on their part, are not insensible to the hope of becoming priors, abbots, knights of St. Anne and of St. Vladimir. If this account be true, then motives far different from religious vocation induce merchants to withdraw into cloisters.

Let us conclude that the Russian people in general furnish to the convents a very weak contingent. The clergy alone gives, proportionately, a hundred times more than the rest of the population. The 140* recruits yearly furnished by it to the convents are subdivided into several classes, which we must be very careful not to confound.

There are, firstly, the seminarists who have not been able to complete their classes. Their career is a broken one. If they quit the ranks of the clergy, conscription there awaits them; in the secular clergy they have no other prospect than that of becoming beadles or sacristans, and even of this all are not sure. They embrace, then, the religious state, and the rather as by this road they can hope to reach the diaconate, or even the priesthood. In any case, the life they will lead in the convent will be less rude than that among the low clergy.

The youths who have finished their course in the seminary have a career open before

---

* 2253 in 16 years give a yearly average of 140.

them: they never dream of donning the cowl. There are, however, some who embrace the monastic life, but they are rare enough. It very frequently happens that a deacon or priest loses his wife. He cannot marry again. If still young, he is admitted to the academy, and reënters the category of which we are about to speak; but if a little older he goes to the convent, sometimes even under compulsion. It must not be forgotten that by one of those inadvertences so frequent in Russian legislation, a priest or deacon who has rendered himself guilty of grave offences, and can no longer exercise his functions, is condemned to the convent, as civilians are elsewhere to the galleys. A seminarist also who has completed his studies, but is not yet ordained, discharges in a seminary the duties of a professor. He is married, say, and loses his wife. If he marry again, he can no longer be ordained, nor even though he remain a widower. Nothing remains for him but to turn monk, unless he prefer to obtain a professorship in a gymnasium or embrace some other career.

Let us now pass to the youths who have done with their classes in one of the four academies of Petersburg, Moscow, Kieff, or Kasan. These, while remaining among the secular clergy, are sure to promptly arrive at the priesthood; but they cannot aspire to the Episcopate; whilst a young man who adopts the monastic life during his course at the academy is morally certain, on quitting it, of being named inspector or préfet of studies in a seminary. At a few years' end he becomes rector or superior, and, provided he himself does not impede his own advancement, he can scarcely fail of attaining the Episcopate.

It is, then, a career, and the numerous details into which our anonymous author enters clearly show us that for all, or nearly all, it is nothing else.

It sometimes happens that these young people not only have no inclination to the religious life, but feel for it a repugnance too strong for even the prospect of a mitre to overcome. On the other hand, difficulty exists in procuring the number of persons necessary for filling positions which cannot be intrusted to monks wholly ignorant. The ecclesiastical authority uses every means to determine a certain number of academic pupils to embrace the monastic life. The strife is sometimes lively. If we are to credit our author, the celebrated Plato, metropolitan of Moscow at the beginning of this century, employed very strange means in these cases. When all methods of persuasion had failed, the recalcitrant student was invited to pass the evening with one of the monks. There he was made to drink until he became intoxicated, when the ceremony constituting religious profession was performed, *i. e.* the taking the habit and receiving the tonsure. On awaking the next morning the unfortunate youth saw beside his bed, instead of the lay garments worn the night before, a monastic habit. Often he fell into a rage, and tore into shreds the tokens of his profession. Then his anger gradually subsided; it was shown to him that what had been done could by no means be undone; and the involuntary monk resigned himself to his fate. All reflection would here be superfluous, and nothing better proves the little account made of vocation about fifty years ago. At the present time recourse is not had to such expedients, but the means now employed are no less singular. The academic pupils do not scruple to frequent the cafés, restaurants, and public-houses of the neighbourhood. There they are sometimes so intoxicated as to lose all consciousness, and are obliged to be carried home to the academy on a hand-barrow. In the slang of the place this act is known as the *Translation of the Relics.** When it is desired to induce one of these students to embrace the religious life spite of his repugnance, they watch

* Перенесеніе честныхъ мощей.

that he become in his turn the hero of one of these orgies. The next day, when he has recovered his senses, the superior summons him to his house, rates him soundly, and informs him of his expulsion. The superior, however, is ready to pardon, to forget everything, if the offender give him evidence of a sincere repentance. Of this he accepts but one proof—the signature of the student to a paper containing a request that he may be allowed to make his religious profession.

Such a fact is of unquestionable gravity. Without doubt 'tis a very lamentable thing that a seminarist should frequent a tavern, and there be allowed to lose his senses; but if the offender were instantly excluded, it would become only an accident, and the superior's responsibility would not be seriously compromised. It is, however, a fact of common occurrence, and hence unpardonable. It is, moreover, joked about, which makes the matter graver still. Finally, what seems quite incredible, the superiors profit by this debauch to force the victim of it to embrace the religious life. That which ought to cause perpetual exclusion gives, on the contrary, admission within the gates of the cloister.

In order to realise these strange manners, let the reader figure to himself, for example, a young English seminarist brought to the seminary in a state of complete insensibility after a drinking bout, and the superior offering him next day his pardon, on condition of his entering the community having the direction of the establishment. Let him then try to understand what the seminary would be, what the clergy, the bishops, the religious congregations, if such a fact were only possible, and let him then measure the distance which separates the Russian clergy from the English.

We must farther remark here on the idea these superiors must have of vocation, of profession, and of the religious life, while admitting to solemn vows such a subject, without transition, without preparation, without amendment.

It is manifest that the fundamental basis of all religious life—vocation—is wanting in the Russian convents. It is not fear of the world and its seductions, the attraction of solitude and prayer, the desire of leading a life of penitence, or of working towards perfection: it is not zeal for souls, love for Jesus Christ, the need of devotion and self-denial, that fill these houses. We must not, however, be deceived. These attractions of the cloister are met with in Russia much oftener than one would be disposed to believe; but Russian convents are unable to satisfy these aspirations. The souls, then, which feel these holy desires do not there present themselves; they do not remain there. Some think to find the realisation of their desires in the East, and go to Mount Athos or to Palestine, but meet there only bitter disappointment. Others go and knock at the convent gate of the Rascolniks, with no better success. Happy they who have learnt that the Catholic Church alone possesses retreats where their dreams can become realities.

After vocation the first stage of the religious life is the novitiate. It is necessary, in order that vocation may be really tested, and that the soul which aspires to take before God irrevocable engagements, may have time to maturely reflect on the grave step it is meditating. It is farther necessary that it should be instructed in the duties of the life which it is going henceforth to lead, that it be formed to the practice of the rules it is about to follow, and of the virtues which it must force itself to acquire; for in all this consists the novitiate. Now, the novitiate in the Russian convents is just as much wanting as is the vocation. The pupils of the theological academies who embrace the religious life make their profession without a novitiate, and it even happens that they attain the Episcopate without ever having lived in a convent.

Here a circumstance occurs which we cannot pass by in silence. According to Russian legislation, as we have seen, women cannot profess before the age of forty; men are allowed to pronounce their vows at thirty, and for the academy pupils the limit has been lowered to twenty-five. These are not the prescriptions of the canon law, but of the civil. It very often happens that a young man has finished his studies before twenty-five, some at twenty-three, some even at nineteen. In order to obtain the authorisation to bring about his profession, instead of procuring a dispensation, false documents are sent stating that he is twenty-five. The religious superiors who send these documents, the bishops and members of the Synod who receive them, perfectly know that recourse has been had to falsehood: both prefer to commit a sin rather than violate an imperial ordinance, which could easily be repealed or dispensed from. But, in their eyes, a ukase is more inviolable than a commandment of God.

As to the seminarists who have not been able to finish their studies, they are not so urged to take irrevocable engagements, but await their thirtieth year; their novitiate is therefore very long. But how is this novitiate passed? The youths receive no instruction in the religious life, do not learn to pray, to examine their consciences, to combat their evil inclinations, nor do they even receive books which might strengthen their good dispositions; no surveillance is exercised over them, no loving advice given them; there is no one to whom to open their hearts, to speak of their temptations, their doubts, their inward troubles. They have no novitiate-master; they do not frequent the Sacraments; their principal occupation is to render service to the monk who is supposed to form them for the religious life. They assist in very long offices, which speak neither to their understanding nor to their heart. The rest of their time is passed in playing and amusing themselves, and often, we must say, their pleasures are anything but religious. When they are weary behind the cloister walls, there is always the means of exit, with or without permission, by day or night.

The monks who do not come from academies and seminaries generally arrive when advanced in age: they are no longer capable of being moulded, even when they wish it. If no novitiate, then no religious life; it cannot be otherwise. Elsewhere, the rule known to all, observed by all, makes each understand every day of his life the truth of the Saviour's words: 'My yoke is easy, and my burden is light.' In the Russian monasteries there is nothing like it. Now there is extreme laxness, now the despotism of a capricious superior; sometimes both at once. Still following our author, as to the rule, it is nowhere observed. The same thing must be said of vows. Take, for example, poverty. There are in Russia a few convents on which community-life has been imposed; there all the wants of the religious are provided for—nothing is one's own. But these monasteries are very few, and the monks who live there in general sigh only for the moment of their being able to quit. In other convents the monks receive lodging, fuel, and nourishment; their clothing, their shoes, and their other necessaries, are at their own expense. The revenues are divided into two parts; the one goes into the treasure-chest, the other is divided among the monks, without forgetting, as we have said, that out of it the superiors have to enrich themselves and their relatives.

The rule forbidding the use of meat to the monks of St. Basil is often put aside, especially by those who ought to set an example. As to drunkenness, our author cites a multitude of facts, each one exceeding its predecessor in sadness. It is not rare to see monks, professors, seminary-directors, archimandrites, the bishops themselves, seeking in drunkenness oblivion of their vexations. After that, one can imagine what becomes of the vow of chastity. Our author has had the good taste not to enter into much detail on this subject; but the little he says suffices to show us that the vow is often broken. We ought, however, to add that, among the bishops and the monks, a certain number are remarkable for their temperance, sobriety, and even for penitence and mortification. We could by no means insist too much on this point: the evil is not in the men, but in the institutions.

As to obedience, at first sight it seems that it is better observed than the other two vows; looked at more closely, it is soon perceived to be an obedience wholly human, devoid of supernatural views, having nothing in common with the virtue so earnestly recommended by all the ascetic authors who have treated of the religious life; often it is only servility.

We have, from our point of view, summed up the facts furnished by the author of the book on the White and Black clergy in special reference to what concerns vocation, novitiate, profession, the observation of vows, and the rule. We have omitted many reflections appearing irrelevant, and discovering, in our opinion, a spirit hostile to religious institutions. We have not dwelt upon faults inseparable from human nature; we are disposed to think that the author has preferred dwelling on the dark sides of the picture, and that he has left in the shade whatever could lessen the gloom. We willingly admit that there are exceptions; it nevertheless results from what we have seen, that the Russian monasteries are in a very bad state.

It remains for us to say a few words on a side of the question on which our author has not touched, but which, however, is very important. We refer to the government of the monasteries, the mode of nomination of the superiors, and their relations with the bishops and the Synod.

A religious Order is an association; those who are members of it propose to themselves a definite end, at which they aim by definite means. It is in verifying the agreement of will, both as to the end and means, between him who presents himself, and the society into which he desires admission, that his vocation can be judged of. On entering the religious life a man renounces everything, abdicates his own right to will; but every sacrifice is joyfully made in view of the end proposed. Abnegation cannot go so far as to sacrifice this end. If you consent to do the will of a superior

in all the details of life, it is on the condition
that he will direct you towards the goal, to
gain which you abandon your own will.   For
this guarantees are necessary, and one of these
is that the superior himself have the same object before *him*, and that for it he also have
sacrificed everything.   In a word, he must be
a member of the association.   This is not all:
he must possess the confidence of his associates,
he must have their approbation; also in every
religious Order the superior is chosen by election.   It is farther necessary that, under the
authority and supervision of the Church, every
religious Order should enjoy a certain independence, that it may be assured of not being
thwarted of its end, but may be able to reach
it by the means the association has chosen.
On the contrary, that a religious order should
come to be governed by a man who is a stranger
to it, would obviously disorganise the whole.
Of this the history of the Church, and especially of the religious orders, is full of examples.

In the Church of the East, which saw the
first religious communities formed in its bosom, these elementary principles have been
always embodied in practice.   To this may be
attributed the enduring prosperity of Mount
Athos.   But you would look in vain for anything like it in the Russian convents.   True,

the Synod might exercise over them a right
of control and inspection, but this does not
exist. The great *laures*, which ought to be
the very abodes of the religious spirit, do not
choose their archimandrites. Borrowing, very
improperly, of Western Europe one of its most
regrettable inventions, the Russian metropolitans are become abbots-commendatory of the
laures, and the bishops of the different sees
equally receive in commandery a monastery
of their dioceses. Everywhere the bureaucracy
names the superiors.* These render an account of their management to the Synod—to
the Synod they are responsible; and when we
say the Synod, we shall hereafter see that we
mean, in fact, the bureau of a minister. Consequently, all these posts, of archimandrites
(abbots), hegoumens (priors), superiors, &c.,
have become the different steps of a career.
For all those who follow it, advancement is the
principal motive; they therefore think only
of making themselves acceptable to those on
whom they depend. All this bureaucratic organisation is at complete variance with the
exigencies and needs of the religious life.

To us it appears demonstrated by all that

---

* The only exception made is in the case of a very small number of convents, chosen among those which have adopted the
community-life.

has gone before, that the monastic life in Russia exists henceforth only in appearance : as to veritable monks—to a religious order properly so called—none such exist. Reforms could indeed be proposed; but so great has been the progress of evil, that reforms the most radical would avail nothing. The day that the clergy in Russia shall cease to exist as a caste—that a secular celibate clergy shall be formed—will be the day when all the monasteries will fall, the whole actual monastic organisation will disappear.

It may be that the convents in which the community-life has been introduced would be susceptible of reform. The monasteries would then have to be divided into two distinct classes. Those not having adopted the community-life should be left to die; the rest, if reformable, should be united into a single congregation, or rather should labour to create several congregations. The *religious* has for his aim to labour for his salvation and perfection—to sanctify himself; but alongside this general aim, he can have a particular one. Some give themselves to the contemplative life, some to foreign missions or to the education of children, to the study and teaching of sacred science, to preaching, to the direction of souls, to care for the sick, &c. &c. Why should not a monastery be chosen as the centre of a congregation for foreign missions ? Another would serve as a centre for an hospital congregation, another for a teaching congregation, another for preachers, and so on. An appeal would be made to those monks who had adopted the community-life, and they would be induced to choose one or other kind of occupation. From among those who would present themselves would be chosen the most pious, the most regular, the most zealous, and the most capable, and they would form the nucleus of new congregations, according to the bias they had manifested. In order to organise these congregations, it would above all be necessary to leave entire liberty to all those who would be willing to enter them, without any other limit as to age than that determined by the canon law. At the same time, the congregations themselves should be very strict as to admissions, very compliant as to dismissions. The best means of preventing laxness creeping into a community is to open reluctantly their doors for those who would come in, and to open them willingly to those who would go out. It would still be necessary that vocation should be seriously tried during a year or two by means of the novitiate, all the novices being gathered together and placed under the direction of a master chosen with the greatest care. The superior should be elected by the members of the congregation, without any interference of the civil authority, of the Synod, or of the bishops. The ecclesiastical authority should confine itself to taking the necessary measures to secure the freedom of the elections. When a congregation shall have developed itself, it will be able to occupy several houses, placed under the authority of one superior-general, each house having a local superior. The particular end proposed to itself by each congregation, the most proper means to attain it, and the practical counsels which experience shall suggest, will be the subject-matter of the special constitutions of each congregation, and become the complement to the Rule of St. Basil, which shall be religiously observed. The formation of congregations, composed of many houses, bound to a common centre, is completely misrepresented by some Russian authors as an innovation borrowed from the Latin Church. We have before seen that the fact formerly existed in Russia, and that its abolition has been for the interest neither of the monasteries nor of the Church.

Here in few words is the scheme of measures to be taken for reforming the monasteries, if they succeed in finding the necessary clements in the convents where community life is practised. We would prefer that, leaving on one side whatever exists, men of good disposition should be allowed to found new communities. We said just now, 'tis not the men who are in fault, but the institutions: the ruin of the monasteries has arisen from the intervention of the bureaucracy, the regulations, and the want of independence. Will liberty raise up new communities? Will it create more order, more regularity, more zeal? The essence of life, the force of religious orders, is the spirit that animates them; and this spirit, where will it be found? We do not know; but we should wish the experiment tried.

Russia has gloriously freed herself from the leprosy of serfdom; she is now on the road to freedom from the yoke of a.harassing bureaucracy, venal and corrupt. The monasteries claim the same reforms: they demand to be emancipated, to live their own life. Take away the multiplied impediments which clog vocations, foundations, and the whole organisation of the religious life, and a great part of the abuses now complained of will disappear. Let the people be free to give alms to the convents, if it seem good to them. You complain that the monks sometimes employ means not warranted by morality to draw to themselves larger gifts. The press and the tribunals are sufficient to repress the disorders which would arise; keep to the common law.

By the side of the monasteries of the official Church leave to the starovères, leave to the Catholics also, the liberty to establish convents; free them from an oppressive guardianship. Justice demands it, your interest agrees with her: you know not all the utility that your convents can draw from a free competition. We wish not to deny that among the Catholic convents there have been some—some there are still—into which abuses have crept, and which laxness has invaded. But go back to the causes, and you will recognise that, almost always, if not always, the root of the evil is in an excessive guardianship on the part of the state. It is the public which sustains communities; it furnishes their members, gives them those material resources without which they could not subsist. The public is not deceived in this matter: it will sustain the useful communities; from the useless it will withdraw its support. If you find exceptions to this law, they are all explained by a single cause—monopoly. With free concurrence, nothing of the kind is to be feared.

CHAPTER III.

ECCLESIASTICAL SCHOOLS.

WE have not to write the history of the ecclesiastical schools in Russia ; we shall, however, say a few words about them.

It is not doubtful that, under Jaroslav and his successors, the sacred sciences were cultivated at Kieff.* It cannot be denied that the Russian Church, in the first days of its foundation, resembled that torch spoken of in Scripture as brightly burning, diffusing all around it light and heat. Little by little the light goes out, the heat withdraws, darkness overspreads minds, and hearts grow cold. Those who are aware that in her beginnings the Russian Church had not broken the bonds which bound her to the Universal Church have no cause for surprise. The regions of the northeast, formerly called Muscovy, and now bearing the name of Great Russia, have shared less

---

* How in Russia, previously to the Mongol invasion (1240), sacred science was extensively and successfully cultivated, see Strahl, *Das gelehrte Russland*, Leipzig, 1828, 8vo. (*Trans.*)

than the south-west, called Little Russia, in this expansion of Christian life, without being completely deprived of it.

In the sixteenth century the darkness became singularly thick; we wish no other proof of this than the celebrated Council of Moscow in 1551, known in history under the name of Stoglaff, or Council of the Hundred Chapters.*

The torch of sacred science was rekindled at Kieff at the contact of the Russian Church with the Catholic, of the Greek rite with the Latin. The first place among the ecclesiastical schools of Russia belongs unquestionably to the Academy of Kieff, founded in 1631 by Peter Moghila. This remarkable man was the son of a hospodar of Walachia, named Simeon Ivanovich. After having studied philosophy and theology at Paris he served with distinction in the Polish army, and particularly signalised himself at the battle of Khotin, 1621. Four years afterwards he embraced the monastic life in the convent of the Crypts at Kieff; in 1628 he was archimandrite of this celebrated *Laure*, and shortly after was called to the see of Kieff. As metropolitan he governed the ununited

---

* Сто—главъ. The decrees of this Council were a few years ago published in London. The Staroveres lean on the authority of this Council, while it is rejected by the official Church.

Church in the States of the Polish Republic
from 1632 to 1646, the date of his death. One
of his first cares had been to found a printing
establishment and a school. This academy,
as it was called, possessed, besides classes for
grammar, chairs of philosophy and theology.
The instruction was given principally in Latin,
but Polish and Little Russian were also used;
the study of Greek was much neglected. The
best students were sent to finish to the College of Lemberg, and to other Catholic schools.
Moghila is the author of a catechism,* or 'exposition of the orthodox faith,' solemnly approved by the Greek Church at the Council
of Jassy in 1643, and at that of Jerusalem in
1672, and equally received by Adrian, patriarch
of Moscow. It may be said that the doctrine of
this catechism, except the question of the *Pope*
and that of the *Filioque*, is Catholic. At Kieff
the *Summa Theologica* of St. Thomas was expounded. The whole organisation of the classes
was traced on that of the Catholic colleges; at
every step we seem to recognise the *ratio
studiorum* of the Society of Jesus; we find
there also the Congregation of the Blessed Vir-

---

* The Russian title is Православное исповѣданіе Каѳолической
и Апостольской Церкви Восточной. This Catechism, in Greek and
Latin, can be seen in Kimmel's *Monumenta Fidei Ecclesiæ Orien-
talis*, Jenæ, 1850. An English translation appeared in London in
1752. (*Trans.*)

gin.* The need of reacting against the growing
ignorance of the clergy soon made itself felt
at Moscow. The celebrated Nicon, one of the
greatest figures appearing in the history of the
Russian Church, undertook to correct the text
of the liturgical books, which had been cor-
rupted by copyists. The resistance encountered
by this reform showed the necessity of having
schools.

The Tsar Feodor had just succeeded his
father Alexis; Nicon was still alive, and one
of his disciples, Simeon of Polotsk, exercised
great influence at court. This Simeon was a
man of merit, born at Polotsk in 1628. Arrived in Russia (1667), after having studied in
Poland, and frequented the Catholic schools,
he had been charged with the education of
Feodor. At the same time he refuted by sub-
stantial writings the errors of the Rascolniks
(dissenters), and composed dramas which were
represented in the apartments of the Princess
Sophia, the daughter of Alexis. When his pupil
mounted the throne, he profited by the credit he
enjoyed to establish a printing-press in the pal-
ace; then he set himself to preach. This was a
bold innovation: before him the most any one had
done was to read some homilies borrowed from

---

* Cf. *Etudes de Théologie, de Philosophie, et d'Histoire*, par les
PP. C. Daniel et J. Gagarin, S.J. (Paris, 1857), vol. i. p. 39.

the holy Fathers; besides, he manifested Catholic tendencies. This was more than enough
to irritate the narrow-minded patriarch Joachim; but Simeon, strong in the friendship
of the Tsar, little feared the wrath of the patriarch, and even thought of depriving him
of the supreme dignity. His plan was to replace at the head of the Russian Church his
master Nicon, who was living in exile, after
having been deposed by order of Alexis. In
order to prevent a schism, Simeon proposed to
the Tsar to create four patriarchs in place of
the four metropolitans, and to put over them
Nicon with the title of pope. It needed but
little to put this project into execution.

The better to explain the situation, let us
farther say that Catholic ideas were under this
reign received at the court with favour. Russia
was maintaining the best relations with Poland.*
Feodor had in 1680 married a young lady of
Polish origin, named Agatha Grouchetzka, to
whom was attributed a leaning towards Catholicism. In consequence of this marriage the
Polish costume was generally adopted at court.
Feodor's foreign policy hinged upon a strict
alliance with Poland, and the formation of a
league against the Turk, into which should

---

* M. Stchebalski affirms it. See русскій ⹁Вѣстникъ (*Russian
Messenger*), Oct. 1863, p. 767.

enter the Emperor of Germany, the Pope, and the Venetian Republic.

It was in these circumstances that Simeon conceived the plan of founding at Moscow a school destined to spread civilisation among both the clergy and the people. Scarcely had he laid its foundations when he died. The only man who could withstand the patriarch thus disappearing, the designs favoured by the Tsar became compromised: he knew not to whom to confide the direction of the school, and, fearing the opposition of Joachim, he hesitated to procure masters from Kieff. He then profited by an embassy he was sending to the Sultan to ask for professors of the patriarch of Constantinople. The embassy set out in 1681; the year following Feodor died, and power passed into the hands of Sophia, the faithful heiress of his policy. In 1684 two Jesuits arrived at Moscow with an ambassador from the Emperor of Germany, and obtained without difficulty permission to remain in that city. To us it not doubtful that Sophia, and Galitzin her minister, had intended to intrust the school to the Jesuits.

About a year after the arrival of the Jesuits, the professors sent by the patriarch of Constantinople made their appearance in the capital. They were two brothers, natives of the Ionian

Isles, who had studied at Venice and Padua.
Their real name was Lycudes;* they changed
it to that of Lykhudes, and by the aid of false
genealogies caused themselves to be recognised
as Bulgarian princes. They were placed at
the head of the new school; the Jesuits, on
their side, had opened another. The two Ionian
monks soon raised a theological question which
inflamed every one, clergy and laity, men and
women. The question was whether, in the
Sacrifice of the Mass, the bread and the wine
are changed into the Body and Blood of Jesus
Christ, by virtue of the words of our Lord,
'This is my Body, this is my Blood,' or by the
invocation of the Holy Spirit, the *Epiclesis*,†
which in the Eastern Liturgy follows the sacra-
mental words. The strife became very lively.
On the one side were all those who inclined to
Catholicism, as Sylvester Medvedeff, superior
of the Convent Zaikonospaski, the monk Sabbas
Dolgui, the prior Innocent, a layman occupying an elevated position, Theodore Stcheglovitoy, and many others. The patriarch and the
two monks, with all those who were hostile to

* See, for biographical notices of these two brothers, Constantine Satha's Νεοελληνικὴ Φιλολογία.—Βιογραφίαι τῶν ἐν τοῖς γράμμασι
διαλαμψάντων Ἑλλήνων ἀπὸ τῆς καταλύσεως τῆς Βυζαντίνης αὐτοκρα-
τορίας μεχρὶ τῆς Ἑλληνικῆς ἐθνεγερσίας, 1453-1821. Ἐν Ἀθήναις (1868),
p. 358. (*Trans.*)

† See on this question Dr. Hoppe's *Die Epiklesis der griech-
ischen und orientalischen Liturgieen, und der römische Consekra-
tions Kanon.* Schaffhausen, 1864.

the Catholics, ranged themselves under the opposite banner.   This war of books and pamphlets lasted as long as Sophia remained at the head of the government.

On August 17th, 1689, broke out the revolution which deprived her of the regency and gave the sovereign power to Peter I.*   Two months had not elapsed before Sophia was shut up in a convent, Galitzin exiled, Stcheglovitoy and Sylvester Medvedeff delivered to the executioner, the Jesuits expelled, and a Protestant visionary named Kuhlman burnt alive.   It is remarkable that Peter I. owed his elevation to Joachim, and to the most ignorant of the clergy : Peter cleared off his debts by persecuting foreigners and those who showed Catholic tendencies. The triumph of the party was not long.   Some months after, the inept patriarch Joachim died ; in 1694 the two monks, denounced and treated as adventurers by Dositheus patriarch of Jerusalem, were sent away from the Slavo - greco - latin Academy. After their departure it lingered on for some time under the direction of their pupils, until in 1702 monks were sent for from Kieff.

Simeon of Polotsk, the brothers Lykhudes, the monks of Kieff, had all derived their know-

* Lefort had founded at Moscow a Masonic lodge, and Peter, it is said, had himself initiated therein.

ledge in the West and in Catholic schools.
They were familiar with the grammar of Al-
varez, the methods of the Jesuits, and the
Summa of St. Thomas. From this an idea
can be formed of the instruction given at the
Moscow Academy: it was an imitation, or if
you like a counterfeit, of the colleges of Catholic Europe. The greater part of the pupils
who frequented it belonged to the clergy neither by birth nor by vocation. On the benches
were seen, according to Smirnoff's history of
this academy, by the side of priests, deacons,
and monks, young men of all conditions, including aristocracy.[*] It appears, however, that
the taste for letters had some difficulty in
spreading itself at Moscow. In 1704, of thirty-
four pupils in philosophy, three names are
found belonging to Great Russia; all the others
to White Russia and Poland.[†] In 1736 we find
that 158 nobles entered the academy, among
whom we distinguish Galitzin, the Dolgoroukys,
and the Obolenskys. The spirit of caste had
not yet penetrated there. The teaching staff
was not recruited from among the pupils of
the house, but from Kieff. We have the list
of rectors, prefects, and professors, from 1703
till 1774: almost all are monks or priests,

---

[*] Smirnoff, История Московской Славяно—Греко—Латинской Ака-
демии Москва (1855), p. 25.   [†] Ibid. p. 81.

natives of the Ukraine or of Poland,* and old pupils at Kieff. What is the origin of this state of things? The answer is easy. At Moscow, scarcely any one completed his studies; sometimes there were in theology but eight students. When they had learnt a little Latin, the pupils went away to seek their fortune elsewhere. A good number of the pupils obtained admittance to the hospital of Moscow, to learn medicine there; others applied themselves to the study of mathematics, which opened to them access to various careers; others still were occupied at the press, at the mint, &c. The governors of the provinces led some away with them to become professors and schoolmasters, &c. Peter I. distributed a good number in the navy and in the guard; others he sent abroad to prosecute their studies. When the Academy of Sciences was founded at Petersburg, attendants were wanted for the course prescribed to it: these were taken from the academy of Moscow. The reforming Tsar had addressed himself to the Jesuits of Prague, to get translated into Russian works on law and dictionaries. Four pupils were chosen to engage in this work under the direction of the Fathers, who went

* Only such names are met with as Krasnopolski, Wisznewski, Miegalewicz, Florinski, Kozlowicz, Liaszczewski, Bronicki, Przybylowicz, Kulczycki, Kolniecki, Konaszewicz, Zaborowski, Rudzinski, Leszczinski, Czarniecki, Jaroszewski, &c.

to study philosophy and letters in another college of the Jesuits. Some students of the academy Peter sent to the mission of Pekin, established by him for a purpose rather political than religious, but which required the services of a certain number of monks having some degree of learning.

In short, the Academy of Moscow was used as a preparatory school, but it does not appear that many priests have proceeded thence. We find in the list of pupils beside the celebrated Lomonossoff, Kostroff, and Petroff, who have made a certain reputation in literature, the Prince Cantemir, Bantysch-Kamenski, the architect Bajanoff; but not a single name reflecting honour on the clergy before that of the metropolitan Platon.

The beginnings of the Academy of Saint Alexander Nevsky, at St. Petersburg, were long subsequent to those of the Academy of Moscow, and much more humble. It was at first only a simple primary school, where children of every condition were admitted. Later it was desired to introduce Latin; but the school could not go on—there was no one to be put at its head. In 1736 recourse was again had to the Academy of Kieff, and two of its pupils succeeded in organising some classes. Setting out from this time, the Academy of Petersburg

followed the steps of that of Moscow, present-
ing however some notable differences. In the
teaching staff we do not see so many monks
from Kieff, and in a little time the pupils are
recruited almost exclusively from the sons of
ecclesiastics. Here also, in consequence of the
paucity of men who had studied in any degree,
the administration takes away a great number
of young men, to launch them in careers the
most diverse, before they have passed their
classes. The Academy of Petersburg, however,
is chiefly a normal school, where are prepared
masters for all newly-founded schools. Some
of the most capable youths are sent abroad to
complete their studies, but are no longer directed to Catholic schools, still less to Jesuit
colleges; they go into Protestant countries.

Such was still the state of things in the
first years of the reign of Catherine II. The
reaction, however, the first symptoms of which
we have just pointed out, was making its way.
The course of theology of Theophane Prokopovich, preserved at first in manuscript, then
committed to the press, profoundly changed
the instruction given in the Russian schools,
and opened the door to Protestantism.* It

* See the proofs of this assertion detailed in our article entitled '*De l'enseignement de la Théologie dans l'Eglise russe*, in the
Etudes, &c. 1st series, vol. i.

must be recollected, that for eleven years, from 1730 to 1741, Russia was governed by the Calvinist Biren, and that the Russian Church was then subjected to a real persecution. To this we must say she opposed but a feeble resistance.

The desire to display sufficiently clearly the first phases of the history of the ecclesiastical schools has perhaps drawn us beyond due limits. To describe all the modifications they have undergone to the present time would be almost impossible, and certainly fastidious: we confine ourselves to indicate the general features, throwing a clearer light on a few important points.

If we designate as the Old that system which prevailed at Kieff, and left so deep an impression on the Academy of Moscow, we shall be able to apply the name New system to the entirety of tendencies which showed themselves under Peter I., and which, in spite of partial checks, never ceased to become daily more evident. In the study point of view, these tendencies may be gathered up into three topics: restricting the teaching of ancient languages in favour of modern ones, of literature in favour of the sciences, of sacred studies in favour of profane. The strife between the two systems presents a double character—instability and uniformity.   All schools are subjected to the same system, and this system is continually being modified.

It would be vain to look in the Russian Church for teaching congregations strongly organised, faithful to their traditions and method: there is no longer any liberty of action left to the bishops in the direction of their seminaries. The ecclesiastical schools, which in their origin were a little independent, and had a spirit peculiar to themselves, are soon seen subject to a central direction which made all establishments pass under the same level.   This central authority, placed in a certain dependence on the Synod, suffered also more or less the influence of the lay element.   The new system attempted to shatter whatever existed; the old sought to keep the positions acquired, and to retake those it had lost.   Hence arose continual swayings, which made themselves felt at once in all the establishments.   Here, beyond a doubt, is one great cause of the weakness of the studies in Russia.   Stability is an indispensable condition of success in matters of education.

Whatever may be our preferences for the ancient methods, we willingly recognise that satisfactory results would have been achieved with the new system.   In our opinion, it would

have somewhat failed in the case of the young
persons leaving these schools; but at least, in
acquiring the knowledge of modern languages,
they would have had access to French or German literature. The study of mathematics and
of the experimental sciences would have given
to their understandings habits of clearness,
order, method, which are not to be despised.
But things do not happen thus. Under the
name *scholastic* all Catholic traditions still sub-
sisting are rejected; the place accorded to
Latin is more and more restricted, without
succeeding in giving to the pupils a sufficient
knowledge of modern tongues; they are made
to study natural history and medicine, to which
will by and by be added rural economy. The
branches of instruction are being multiplied,
and that fatal path entered on of encyclopædic
studies, which overload the memory of children with a mass of superficial information,
without forming their judgment or developing
their intellect. And this organised chaos is
still subject to continual changes. Between
the studies of childhood and those which terminate education, there is a necessary bond.
What profit can be gained from courses of
study by a seminarist, who has not, in inferior
classes, obtained the knowledge which these
courses presuppose? How will you obtain good

professors, if you demand of them to teach what they have not previously learnt? And yet these are the results arrived at by this uniformity, to which is attached so much value.

Speaking of the monks, we observed how necessary it is to allow teaching congregations to organise and develop themselves freely. The history of the Russian seminaries plainly shows that there is a blank, and that it could not too soon be filled up. Suppose there are several congregations to-day, one of which keeps the traditions of Peter Moghila, another those of Simeon of Polotsk, a third those of Theophane Prokopovich, whilst others incline to the new system; each has its own methods, its own nursery for its professors. This variety maintains emulation, but the *esprit de corps* secures stability. Allow the bishops to intrust their seminaries to a congregation of their own choice, and it will furnish those professors whom you do not succeed in producing.

All the books, all the journals that treat of the ecclesiastical schools in Russia, testify to the hatred more or less manifest against the monks: people are indignant at seeing them at the head of the seminaries, and would displace them. In our opinion, people are above all against the monks because they show themselves little favourable to innovation; but, whilst admitting that the grievances articled against them may be well founded, these grievances would disappear before the reforms we have suggested. Better still: the great, the true reason which necessitates the maintenance of the monks in the seminaries is, that they alone represent the celibate clergy, and that it would be very strange indeed to see the functions of rector or prefect discharged by a father of a family, occupying, with his wife and daughters, an apartment among young men, and looking for sons-in-law among the seminarists. Let there be formed a secular celibate clergy, and nothing will prevent seminaries being directed by secular priests.

No! the root of the evil is not there, where they persist in pointing to; it is in this central direction, in this kind of ministry for the education of the clergy placed in double dependence on the Synod and the State, but where the influence of the State is predominant. And, strange to say, whilst the direction of the ecclesiastical schools passes more and more into the hands of the laity; whilst the instruction given in the seminaries tends more and more to become secular,—clerical influence is made to appear on the side least advantageous to it. We have seen that formerly young men of all classes assembled on the benches of the

Academy of Moscow; to-day the ecclesiastical
schools are exclusively reserved to the children
of the tribe of Levi. In the first chapter of
this work we said what we thought of a like
state of things, and the reforms which in our
opinion it demanded. Between the maintenance of caste and the organisation of the ecclesiastical schools there is a connection that must
be broken. Now, of all the means that can be
employed to this end, one of the most efficacious
in our eyes would be the formation of teaching
congregations, whose schools should be open
to all classes of society.

These reflections will acquire new force,
taken in connection with the most salient facts
in the history of the ecclesiastical schools.

A commission established by Catherine II.
(September 7th, 1781) to endow Russia with
new schools, took as a model the institutions
which Joseph II. had just then created in Austria, and borrowed from them the organisation
of the normal schools. Its work having been
approved by Catherine (August 5th, 1786), the
Synod hastened to adapt the same plan to the
schools of the clergy. We then find that mathematics, experimental physics, mechanics,
and natural history entered into the scheme of
ecclesiastical study. The seminary of Nevsky
took the name of General Seminary : each dio-

cese was to send thither two of its best pupils.
Here the influence of Joseph II. is perceptible.

Under Paul I. a reaction is seen. He decides (December 18th, 1797) that there shall
henceforth be four ecclesiastical academies or
faculties of theology ; that besides the instruction common to all the seminaries, complete
courses of philosophy and theology in Latin, as
well as of eloquence and physics, shall be organised there, and that Greek, Hebrew, German, and French shall be taught. Two years
are devoted to philosophy, three to theology.
During these three years the students must also
occupy themselves with ecclesiastical history,
with holy Scripture, moral and polemical theology, the canon law, and the obligations of
curés. It is difficult not to recognise in these
dispositions the influence of Father Gruber,
general of the Jesuits.*

This plan, which seems borrowed from the
Catholic seminaries, was modified no later than
the following year. In 1804 another was made,

---

* At this time Father Gruber was in great favour with the
Emperor Paul. M. Tchistovich, in his History of the Ecclesiastical
Academy of St. Petersburg (Исторія С. Петербургской Духовной Академіи. Спб. 1857, 8vo), mentions a canonical dissertation on the
authority of the Pope, composed in 1800 by the Archimandrite
Eugeny, prefect of the academy, on the occasion of a project of
reunion of the Churches presented by Father Gruber. The dissertation was remitted by the Metropolitan Ambrose to the Imperial
Cabinet. The archimandrite, according to Tchistovich, did this

giving more time to the mathematical and physical sciences, and creating a course of natural history. The first four years are spent in classes for grammar, the fifth embraces logic, rhetoric, universal history and geography, natural history, the Greek, French, and German languages (begun in the first years), medicine, and ecclesiastical computation. During the sixth year the studies are the history of philosophy, geometry, trigonometry, theoretical and practical physics, eloquence, the same languages as the year before, and medicine. Finally, the seventh and last course comprises *ecclesiastical history, dogmatic theology, ecclesiastical archæology, hermeneutics and exegesis, sacred eloquence, moral theology, geometry and trigonometry, physics, Greek, French, and German.* The class-time is eight hours per day. We would gladly believe that this course lasted more than a year; but, in truth, one asks oneself if the authors of this programme had *themselves* ever studied.

Instruction in medicine began in 1802; it

---

by the order of Paul himself. This is a fact as curious as it is important. We ought to declare that we had no knowledge of it. It is to be desired that the project presented by Father Gruber, and the answer of the Archimandrite Eugeny, should be sought for in the archives, and published. Eugeny died Metropolitan of Kieff. The late M. Moroschkin asserted to me that Eugeny's answer had been found at Kieff.

was laid aside in 1808, to be resumed later, and again abandoned (February 1866).

On November 29th, 1807, the Emperor Alexander I. resolved once more to reform the ecclesiastical schools, and charged with this task a committee, the soul of which was Michael Speranski. We cannot refrain from saying a few words of this personage.

Born in 1772 in the diocese of Vladimir, Michael Gramatin was the son of a poor country priest. He was first admitted to the seminary of Vladimir, and there the ambitious youth took the name Speranski, thus indicating by a word borrowed from the Latin the high hopes he nourished in his heart. From Vladimir he passed to the seminary of Nevski, where he completed his studies in theology, and became afterwards professor of sacred eloquence, of mathematics, and soon also of physics; to these three chairs he later joined the duties of prefect of studies. They pretend that he was equal to everything. To speak the truth, he united in himself two qualities which rarely meet together—great facility and great application to work; but on seeing him discharging three or four functions, each of which would suffice to absorb the entire attention of one man, one can scarcely help being reminded of that tailor who was cited before Sancho Panza's tribunal in the Isle of Barataria, and who, with a piece of cloth hardly enough to make *one* coat, had, at the request of his employer, made five thereof, but so small that each could clothe only a doll. However, all these occupations failing to 'fill up' Speranski's day, he obtained the place of private secretary to Prince Kourakin. For some time he lived with this statesman, taking his meals with the servants, and going to the monastery of Nevski to discharge his duties. Shortly afterwards Kourakin obtained from the metropolitan the dismission of Speranski, for whom he procured a place in his own office. This occurred December 24th, 1796. On the 19th of March 1801 Speranski was Secretary of State. He was not slow in acquiring the entire confidence of the Emperor Alexander, and in becoming the most influential person in the empire. He had already introduced very great modifications into the administration of state, and was preparing a complete reorganisation, when, on March 17th, 1812, he was arrested, and relegated first to Nijni, then to Perm. Some years after, Alexander called him to employment of considerable importance; but the first confidence returned no more. Nicholas charged him to make a collection of all ukases and a systematic abstract of them, to which was given the name of code.

He died in 1839, a chevalier of St. Andrew, decorated with the title of Count, and possessed of a fair fortune.

This extraordinary man has more than one title to our notice. The son of a priest, educated in the schools of the clergy, professor and prefect of studies in one of the first seminaries of Russia, he exercised a notable influence on the reorganisation of ecclesiastical instruction in 1809.

In this, as in everything he touched, we recognise the presence of a mind more capacious than deep; the love of regulation, of bureaucracy, of centralisation; schemes of perfect symmetry which have no regard to the ground on which it is proposed to build, and where the substance of things is continually sacrificed to their form. These are only façades, behind which there is nothing; or rather, the only serious thing about it is, that they subject all the schools of the clergy to an administration dominated by the influence of the laity. There were to be academies, seminaries, district schools, parish schools; and everything should terminate in the central direction which gave the impulse to everything, and reduced the members of this magnificent hierarchy to simple wheelwork destined to transmit motions they did not themselves possess.

Here, in few words, is the organisation given to the academies. The pupils drawn from the seminaries ought to have finished their philosophy, to know Latin, and one of the three languages, Greek, German, or French, and to be not more than twenty-two years old: the length of the course was six years. The different subjects for instruction and authors adopted were the following:

I. Dogmatic Theology. Author: Theophane Prokopovitch, abridged by Irenæus Fialkovski (Latin). Auxiliary authors: 1. Fr. Buddæi Institutiones Theologiæ Dogmaticæ; 2. Holtazii Examen Theologicum Acroamaticum; 3. Turretini Institutio Theologiæ Elenchicæ; 4. Sardagna, Opera Theologica.

II. Moral Theology. Authors: 1. Mgr. Theophylact, Instruction Orthodox, pt. ii. (in Russ); 2. Schuberti et Buddæi Institutiones Theologiæ Moralis.

III. Polemic Theology. Authors: Buddæus, Ernest Schubert, Lang.

IV. Hermeneutics. Authors: Mgr. Ambrose (Russ), Buddæus. Auxiliary Authors: the Fathers of the Church, Osiander, Tirinus, Veith, Dom Calmet.

Note. The Professor of Theology knows it: the Kingdom of God is not in word, but in power; the letter killeth, the spirit alone giveth life. Hence, in reading the Holy Scripture, we cannot always be satisfied with the literal or elementary sense.

(With a like note the professor is singularly at his ease: the literal sense will not embarrass him; the door is open to Strauss and his fellows.)

V. Homiletics. Authors: Buddæus, Tellus.

VI. Canon Law. The Kormtchaïa (in Russ), *i.e.* the Pedalion : 1. Beveridge's Pandects ; 2. Bingham's Antiquitates ; 3. The Notitia Ecclesiastica of Cabasutius ; 4. Cavei Historia ; 5. Historia Alexandri Natalis ; 6. Archæologia Posseri Græca ; 7. Buddæi Ecclesia Romana cum Ruthenica irreconciliabilis ; 8. Finally, the ' Spiritual Regulation' of Peter I., with all the ecclesiastico-political legislation that followed.

VII. Philosophy. Complete course of Metaphysics, the History of Philosophy in its whole extent, Physics theoretical and practical.

VIII. Æsthetics and Eloquence. Precepts : Blair, Rollin, Levisac, Bouterweck, Cicero, Horace, Longinus, Quinctilian, Dionysius of Halicarnassus, Laharpe, Gerard ; selections from D'Alembert, Montesquieu, Marmontel, Fenélon, Cardinal Maury, Chateaubriand, Burke, Batteux, Meiners, Eschenburg. Models : Demosthenes, Cicero, Titus Livy, Tacitus, Sallust, Quintus Curtius, Pliny the younger ; St. J. Chrysostom, St. Augustine, the Holy Bible ; Pascal, Bossuet, Fénelon, Flechier, Bourdaloue, Massillon, Saurin.

IX. Physics and Mathematics. 1. Elements of Geometry as far as conic sections inclusive ; Arithmetic, Algebra ; 2. Curvilinear Geometry, Differential and Integral Calculus ; 3. Physics, Mathematics.

X. Historical Sciences. Auxiliary Sciences : 1. Chronology, Ancient Geography, Geography of Russia (two years) ; 2. Biblical and Ecclesiastical History, Christian Antiquities, Russian History ; 3. Universal History.

XI. Languages. 1. Greek, not on the same level as Latin (1st year, Xenophon, Thucydides, Herodotus, Plutarch ; 2d, Demosthenes, Æschines, Lysias, Isocrates, St. Basil, St. Gregory Nazianzen, St. John Chrysostom; 3d, Plato, Aristotle ; 4th, Homer, Hesiod, Aristophanes ; 5th,

Sophocles, Æschylus, Euripides; 6th, Theocritus, Bion, Anacreon, Pindar); 2. Hebrew; 3. German and French.

The choice of authors is noteworthy. For theology, it is specially Buddæus, a Protestant theologian. What would have been said by Stephen Javorski and Theophylact Lopatinski, those two athletes who fought against him with so much vigour? How will any one set about the task of convincing us that their faith was the same as that of the Synod of 1809? This first course counted seventy-eight pupils: eight became bishops, and one of these, Mgr. Gregory Posnikoff, died some years ago metropolitan of St. Petersburg; another, Koutnevich, was a member of the Synod; then a considerable number of priests, who have been more or less influential by their teaching in the chairs of the academies and seminaries, or by the works they have published. We content ourselves with naming Pavski. Ought we to be astonished at finding Protestant ideas in the Russian clergy?

When it became a question of *converting to orthodoxy* the Prussian princess destined to marry him who was one day to be the Emperor Nicholas, the priest charged to instruct the neophyte received from the Synod instructions, in which, among other things, we read as follows: ' In the exposition of the dogmatical teaching of the Greco-Russian Church, it must be explained with the greatest care that this Church recognises the word of God contained in holy Scriptures as the *only* and *perfectly sufficient* rule of faith and of Christian life, and as the *sole* measure of truth; that it doubtless reverences the tradition of the primitive Church, but only so far as it is found accordant with holy Scripture; and finally, that from this pure tradition it draws not new dogmas of faith, but edifying *opinions*, as also *directions*, for ecclesiastical discipline.'*

Thus spoke the Synod in 1816. We hope that M. Yanycheff, charged with the instruction of the Princess Dagmar, received other instructions. In any case, we can thus see what progress Protestantism had made in the Synod at the beginning of this century. The priest armed with these instructions ought to deliver them thus: 'Princess, we keep, it is true, a crowd of ceremonies and observances which shock you; we are obliged to conform thereto, from fear of irritating an ignorant and bigoted people; but at heart we do not hold them, and we are as good Protestants as the King of Prussia. Be pleased, then, to condescend to conform to the usages of a people over whom you may be called to reign, and

* See Nic. Tourgueneff, *La Russie et les Russes,* vol. iii. p. 304.

in your inmost conscience remain what you are.'

The new regulation distributed the day among four classes of two hours each. The members of the commission had not, indeed, then gone beyond the grammatical courses, inasmuch as they imagined that in theology it is possible to have eight hours of classes every day.

STUDIES. MORNING.	Monday.	Tuesday.	Wednesday.	Thursday.	Friday.	Saturday.
Eloquence . . .	9-10	. .	. .	. .	9-10	. .
History	. .	. .	9-10	. .	. .	11-12
Mathematics. . .	. .	11-12	. .	11-12	. .	. .
Philosophy . . .	. .	9-10	. .	9-10	. .	9-10
Theology	11-12	. .	11-12	. .	11-12	. .
AFTERNOON.						
Eloquence . . .	. .	. .	. .	. .	. .	. .
History	5-6	. .	. .	5-6	. .	. .
Mathematics. . .	. .	. .	5-6	. .	5-6	. .
Theology	. .	5-6	. .	. .	. .	. .
Greek	3-4	. .	. .	. .	3-4	5-6
Hebrew	. .	3-4	. .	3-4	. .	. .
French and German	. .	. .	3-4	. .	. .	3-4

When this mechanism was put in motion, it was of course seen to be unable to work. It was then declared that theology, philosophy, sacred eloquence (less the theory or æsthetics), ecclesiastical history, and Greek, were obligatory on every one; that, for the other branches of instruction, students should choose between mathematics and history, between Hebrew and a living language; and the whole duration of the classes was reduced to six hours.

It was quite natural that embarrassment should be experienced in finding professors, and that the authorities should not be very particular notwithstanding. How can we fail to be surprised at seeing certain selections? Let us give an example.

At this time there was abroad an ungowned Capuchin, who had embraced Protestantism and married; but who had been divorced from his first wife and had married another. His manners were dissolute; he believed in nothing, and had obtained for himself a certain reputation in Freemasonry. If he were not connected with the *Illuminati* of Bavaria, he yet much resembled them; his name was Fessler. This was the man to whom they chose to offer a chair in the reorganised ecclesiastical academy. They began by intrusting him with the teaching of Hebrew; finding soon that this did not suffice, they gave him the chair of philosophy.

Everybody in Paris still remembers the feeling produced there by the nomination to the Hebrew chair of a man who had publicly testified his nonbelief in the divinity of Jesus Christ. Yet, M. Renan's antecedents are not those of Fessler, nor is the College of France a semi-

nary. How is it then, that, in a country pretending such jealousy for its orthodoxy, the
instruction of the future pastors of the Russian
Church was confided to such a man as the latter ?   It is not my task to explain it : I know
only that Speranski got Fessler to initiate him
into the mysteries of Freemasonry, and declared
himself his protector. He was given an apartment in the neighbourhood of the *Laure*, and,
in the very interior of the academy, a chamber
where he passed a great part of the day in familiar conversation with the seminarists. It is
sad to say so, but these young men were en-
raptured with this singular professor.   Let us
hasten to add that such a scandal excited the
zeal of the Bishop of Kalouga, Theophylact Rou-
sanoff; and in spite of the efforts of Speranski,
at the end of five months Fessler was obliged
to resign.   Speranski was eager to procure for
him another place in the Law Commission.*
In the memoirs left by Fessler he relates that
the persecutions of which he was the object

---

* Some years later the Emperor Alexander wished that the
Protestants of his states had bishops, like the Anglican and Swedish
Churches. Being nominated Protestant Bishop of Saratoff, Fessler
got himself consecrated in Finland ; afterwards exercised jurisdiction over the Protestants at Saratoff, Astrakan, Voronej, Tam-
boff, Rezan, Penza, Simbirsk, Kasan, and Orenburg. In one of
his pastoral visits he lost his second wife, whom he hastened to
replace by another. He made pretensions to apostolical succession, and used to ordain priests.

had for their motive the preference given by
him to the Platonic over the peripatetic philosophy. But, without entering into the examination of his teaching, it is evident that
the choice of such a man for professor in
a seminary was sufficient to alarm the conscience of any bishop having any anxiety about
doctrine.

This alone, better than long reasonings, en-
lightens us as to the disposition of Speranski,
and as to the spirit in which he had conceived
his reforms. We know well that, after his
disgrace, he affected the semblance of piety.
He translated the *Imitation*, willingly read the
holy Fathers, assisted in the offices, partook
of the sacraments, and in his conversation and
correspondence frequently spoke of God, Providence, and of the life hereafter. But it would
be difficult to say what religion he had in his
inmost heart. Was he orthodox, Protestant,
or Deist? We know only that his was a soul
without loftiness, knowing no other motive
than ambition. Speranski lavished the lowest
flatteries on such a man as Araktchéïeff. Speranski, who passed as the first jurisconsult of
the empire, put his signature to the end of the
sentence which condemned the conspirators
of the 14th December 1825, although in this
process the forms of justice had been outrage-

ously violated. 'He is a great hypocrite,' said of him Count Cancrin, finance-minister of the Emperor Nicholas. Baron Korff has inserted this expression in his Life of Speranski, and it will doubtless be the judgment of posterity.

In stopping to notice the physiognomy of Speranski, we do not swerve from our subject.

It is worth remarking, that *holy* Russia is exposed to have ministers of this temper, and they can exercise an incontestable influence over the Church and her doctrine, by the choice of subjects, by the direction given to studies. It is a farther argument against the central direction of the schools of the clergy.* Fessler is not the only Protestant who has taught in

---

* There is a singular parallelism between the destinies of Speranski and Fessler. In 1810 they are both at the apogee of their fortune; in 1811 Speranski was precipitated from his pinnacle of greatness, and banished to Nijni, then to Perm. Some months before, Fessler had quitted Petersburg and withdrawn to the banks of the Volga, into an estate of Zlobin, brother-in-law of Speranski; sent away by Zlobin Feb. 25th, 1813, he took refuge at Saratoff. On Oct. 3d, 1815, he established himself at Sárepta; Jan. 1st, 1816, his emoluments were suppressed: he was obliged to sell his books, and to have recourse to his friends in Germany for the means of living. Soon, however, the wind changes. On Aug. 30th of the same year Speranski is named Governor of Penza; Aug. 20th, 1817, Fessler is restored to his appointments; March 22d, 1819, Speranski becomes Governor-general of Siberia; July 8th, Fessler is authorised to reënter Petersburg; and on Oct. 25th a Protestant bishopric is erected for him at Saratoff. In thus following the vicissitudes of fortune in the lives of these two men, we can verify the greater or less amount of credit which the Freemasons enjoyed.

the Academy of Petersburg. After him came
two of his co-religionists—John von Horn, who
succeeded him as professor of philosophy and
Hebrew, and Christian Frederic Graefe, who
long filled the chair of Greek. We quite
understand that the professors of the faculty
of theology of Dorpat should be Protestants;
this is quite natural; but we do not understand
confiding to Protestants the care of forming
the *orthodox* clergy. What has been the result ? We have already observed that Protestant ideas and doctrines have penetrated the
Russian clergy; at every step we find proofs
of it ; and perhaps the instructions given by
the Synod to the priests charged to lead the
German princesses to exchange their Protestantism for *orthodoxy* are nearer the truth than
is thought. Without doubt the doctrines professed by the Greek and the Russian Church
were not the least Protestant in the world;
but it cannot be disputed that, for a century
past, a work has been going on among the
Russian clergy, separating them more and more
from their old traditions, and drawing them
every day nearer and nearer to the Protestant
ministers.

Let us return to the ecclesiastical academy
of Nevsky. The organisation of the studies
was so vicious that it was obliged to undergo

radical modifications. The course, reduced to four years, was divided into two sections—two years of philosophy, and two of theology. With philosophy were studied Latin, literature, universal history, and mathematics; with theology, ecclesiastical history, Christian antiquities, chronology, sacred geography, and Russian literature. Holy Scripture, Greek, Hebrew, French, and German, were common to both sections. The lessons of holy Scripture became reading of the Bible, with commentaries; the Old Testament was read with philosophy, the New with theology. Programmes were at the same time drawn up for the different branches of instruction. The course of theology must embrace: 1. Introduction to theology; 2. Hermeneutics; 3. Dogmatic theology; 4. Moral theology; 5. Polemic theology; 6. Patristic; 7. Orthodox liturgy; 8. Pastoral; 9. Homiletics; and 10. Canon law. No serious man will imagine that a young man could learn in two years everything enumerated in this programme, and at the same time the other matters just indicated. What is the result? The students are profound in nothing; they are given only small abridgments, which serve merely to overload the memory. In the great Catholic schools the course of philosophy runs for three years, that of theology for four years, which makes the time seven years instead of four, and the branches of instruction are much less numerous.

Examining the programme of 1814, one is at once struck with the puerile desire of symmetry, which has nothing in common with true science, and which seems to be a heritage of Speranski's mind. Here, for example, is the programme of the course of dogmatic theology:

I. On God:
    1. Knowledge of God.
    2. Unity of God.
    3. The Holy Trinity.

II. ,, the Creator.
III. ,, Providence.
IV. ,, Angels.
V. ,, Man:
    1. On man's nature and state before the fall.
    2. ,, his fallen state.
    3. ,, ,, Restoration.
    4. ,, the Requisites to salvation.
    5. ,, ,, Means of salvation.
    6. ,, ,, Church:
        a. In itself.
        b. On the Sacraments.
        c. ,, Hierarchy.
        d. ,, Laws of the Church.

VI. On the last state of man and the world.

At first sight, a theologian is shocked at the want of proportion presented by this table.

In these six great divisions, there is one which demands thrice the space of the other five. The section on *God*, even joining to it that on *Providence*, presents important lacunæ. It is inexplicable why the sections on the *Hierarchy* and the *Church* are separated the one from the other. It is equally surprising to see thrown into one subdivision the subject of the *Sacraments*, which comprehends eight parts; one on *sacraments* in general, and seven relating severally to the sacraments in particular. Now, among the sacraments, the treatises on the *Eucharist*, on *Penitence*, and on *Matrimony*, have an importance of the first order.

We search this table in vain for the vast beautiful treatises *De Actibus humanis, de Gratia, de Virtutibus, de Peccatis.* It will perhaps be said that they are referred to morality; but it is one thing to consider these matters in a moral point of view, and another to consider them in the dogmatic. And if this omission is admissible in a diocesan seminary, it cannot be accepted in the case of a house of high studies; for it must not be lost sight of, that the four ecclesiastical academies of Russia, and especially that of Petersburg, form the rank most distinguished in theological instruction. *And this high course occupies two years!* and the author to-day adopted is Mgr. Macaire,

who wrote in Russian! What would be said
in France of a seminary where theology should
take two years, and that in French? If there
are any such, they do not boast of them; in
any case, they are not faculties of theology, or
anything approaching thereto.

For moral theology, the Academy has remained faithful to *Buddæus*; for polemical, to
Schubert.

We have not information sufficient for us
to form an opinion of the manner in which
philosophy is taught in the Academy of Petersburg; but the history of this academy, from
which we have borrowed many facts and hints,
has been written by M. Tchistovich, professor
of philosophy in that institution;* and we are
not a little surprised to see his declaration
that, in the ecclesiastical academies, the teaching of philosophy has for its object to demonstrate the feebleness of human reason, and its
inability to discover truth by its own forces,
without the light of revelation. If this is not
traditionalism, I know not now where to look
for it. Beyond doubt, rationalists are quite
wrong in pretending that human reason, left
to its sole force, can attain every kind of truth;

* Исторія С. Петербурской духовной Академіи, сочиненіе ординар-
наго Профессора С. Петербурской духовной Академіи Иларіона Чисто-
вича. Спб, 1857, 8vo.

but to conclude of it that it is impotent to know truth, is to sap the foundation of reason and faith, philosophy and theology.

The study of universal history was not obligatory from 1814 to 1844 ; in the latter year it became obligatory. In 1842 the course of Russian history was extended to all students ; in 1851 it was divided. Russian history was taught to the pupils in philosophy, Russian church history to the pupils in theology. In 1844 the study of physics and mathematics was rendered equally obligatory. Until 1842 eight hours weekly were devoted to these sciences; in 1845 four hours and a half sufficed ; since 1849 they occupy six hours. At an epoch not specified, but which can be conjectured, the professor of history was warned to beware of two rocks—an excessive criticism and fatalism. To these two recommendations, very reasonable in themselves, was added a third, of which I am unwilling to deprive the reader : ' Avoid an inconsiderate political direction, which could bring forth in young minds a tendency to dream and to judge of *what ought not to be submitted to their judgment.*' From this one can imagine what the course of history must be.*

* In illustration of the sentence in italics, we quote the following explanation of the autocratical power of the Tsar which

In the primitive plan instruction in Latin had been wholly laid aside, on the supposition that the young men on leaving the seminary would be sufficiently acquainted with the language. The event, it appears, did not justify this trial, and in 1847 two classes in Latin weekly were established. In these were expounded Lactantius, Cicero, T. Livy, Tacitus, Virgil, Horace; that is to say, what the students were thought to have seen in the grammar-classes was here repeated. Very modest this!

We have seen above the selection of authors to be read in Greek. This programme, which places Thucydides in the first year, is evidently the work of men who were ignorant of Greek. They soon returned to wiser ideas. The course was divided into two sections, the first comprising the beginners; to the second were explained Homer, Lucian, Apollodorus, Diodorus Siculus, Pausanias, Xenophon, &c.; then they touch on Æschylus, Sophocles, Euripides; lastly, they pass to Demosthenes, Isocrates and the Fathers of the Church. The

---

is alluded to in the 1st article of the Russian Code: 'His Majesty is a monarch autocratic, who has not to give reason for his actions to anybody on earth, but has the power and authority, as Christian sovereign, to administer his state and country according to his own will and discretion.' (*Trans.*)

study of French and German has also become obligatory; so that a return has imperceptibly been made to almost the very programme of 1809, which was found too full in 1814.

It is seen, then, that there is one thought in the plan of 1797, and another in that of 1809: the first belonged to the Jesuits, the second to the Freemasons; the rest was mere routine.

In 1863 a new reform was tried. Instead of dwelling on it, we prefer giving here our own views on the matter.

We should like to see in all the seminaries two years allotted to philosophy, and three to theology: the instruction should be given in Latin. It is even to be wished that the use of scholastic disputation be revived. During the theological course the whole attention should be expended on dogma and morality; all else should be accessory. There should be only three hours of class daily, and at most two or three hours weekly for accessories, so distributed that one year should be devoted to ecclesiastical history, another to canon law, a third to holy Scripture. The academies, to which should be admitted only those young men who have finished their studies in the seminaries, should be true faculties of theology. There all the branches of sacred science should be taught, with all the fulness they admit of; there should be formed the men destined to become professors in the seminaries. By permitting the best pupils to spend some years in foreign travel, good professors of faculties would be prepared. These professors should evidently not be taken from among Protestants; the formation of the clergy can be entrusted only to men whose doctrine gives every security. We would, farther, that that mixture of monks, secular priests, and laymen, should be renounced. If the reforms proposed by us were adopted, one or two academies might be reserved for the secular celibate clergy; the others should be confided to monks; and if there existed two or three separate teaching congregations, there would be no disadvantage in introducing into different academies different congregations. As to the choice of authors, it is high time to lay aside Buddæus and the other Protestant theologians. Similarly it would be necessary to subject to a careful examination the books published by members of the Russian clergy, who have allowed themselves to be drawn towards Protestantism. At the head of these is Theophane Prokopovich. It should be seen what was thought of him and his doctrine by Etienne Javorski and Theophylact Lopatinski. For this purpose it would be very useful to have reprinted the great work of Javorski, published by Lopatinski, and entitled *The Stone of Faith.** It is a refutation of Protestantism, which ought to be placed in the hands of every student of theology.

It rarely happens that we are of the same opinion as the anonymous author of the book on *The White and Black Clergy;* this is one more reason for seizing the occasion of citing him when we agree with him. The chair of dogmatic theology ought not to be an appendage to the rectorship; quite on the contrary: these two employments are incompatible. Teaching demands men who devote themselves wholly to it, and remain each in his own speciality. If they so remain long, they will be but the better for it. A professor who has for any length of time occupied a chair can rarely exchange it for another without inconvenience; and he who has lived a few years without teaching can scarcely ever return to it again. These considerations ill agree with the career followed by the poorly-instructed monks in Russia. Whatever employ is confided to them, they consider it only as a lower ladder to raise them to a higher. With this system good professors will never be obtained. A semi-

* Камень Вѣры.

nary superior, who has shown some aptitude
for administration, who possesses virtues necessary for governing men, and fulfils besides
the other conditions required, can be with advantage promoted to the episcopate. On the
other hand, the bishop being not only a pastor
but a doctor, we understand that the episcopate receives a theologian of merit; but, as a
general rule, it is to be wished that good professors keep to teaching, and make it exclusively their ambition to become eminent in
their line.

Hitherto we have been chiefly occupied
with teaching; we must now study another
aspect of the question,—the administration of
houses destined for the training of the clergy,
the discipline observed there, and the education received by candidates for the priesthood.

We have seen that the administration of
these establishments, centred at first in the hands
of the commission on ecclesiastical schools, was
afterwards placed among the functions of the
Synod, but that really it is exercised by the
central direction, which depends on the chief
procurator at least as much as on the supreme
*council** of the Russian Church. In 1863 a
new regulation was published. Judging of it

* As to the applicability of the term 'council' to the Synod,
see *infra*, p. 219.

by the attacks of the philo-slave journal, *The Day*,* and by those of our anonymous author, it would contain notable and serious ameliorations. For the first time, the diocesan bishop is invested with the rights belonging to him over his seminary. Under the supervision of the central direction, he exercises over this nursery of his clergy a veritable authority. The rector, named at Petersburg on the bishop's presentation, is assisted by a pedagogic council, composed of the prefect of studies or inspector, of six professors, and of three or four priests, whom the city clergy choose from their midst. The powers of this council are very extended, but at the same time the rector's authority over the whole *personnel* of the house is entire. Until now the professorships in the seminaries were, in the majority of cases, held by sons of ecclesiastics, who, after having terminated their studies at the seminary or at the academy, remained laymen. To entrust the education of the young Levites to men who thus testify their aversion from the vocation to the ecclesiastical state, was not the way to preserve this vocation in the pupils. The new regulation has understood this, and the men of this category will be separated from the seminaries.

These dispositions, so reasonable, are vio-

* День.

lently criticised by the philo - slave journal.
Now what does it ask? Separation from the
monks, teaching confided to the laity, all professors without distinction called to sit in a
pedagogic council, the rector and the inspector
chosen by ballot by the staff of professors. It
is indignant at the authority confided to the
bishop and the rector, and in it sees only the
triumph of despotism. (*The Day*, 1863, Nos.
41 and 46.) Verily we cannot believe our
eyes. These fiery athletes of *orthodoxy* speaking a language which seems borrowed from the
extremest republicans when it is a question of
an educational establishment, or of a seminary!
No study is more curious than this question of
ecclesiastical places of education: masks fall
off, and every man betrays his most secret
thoughts. The philo-slaves speak like freemasons; they have the same hatreds and the
same preferences.

We by no means wish to constitute ourselves the advocates of the Russian clergy; but
how comes it that these men, who inscribe the
word *orthodoxy* on their banner, show themselves
animated with such hostile sentiments towards
the clergy? How can we help recalling that
these same men have placed the supreme authority of their Church, not in the œcumenical
council — that is to say, in the assembly of

bishops—but in the universal suffrage of the people, sanctioning or rejecting the decrees of the councils? The question is the education of young men who are to be clothed with the priesthood, the instructing them in sacred knowledge and revealed truth; and it is not necessary, forsooth, that the bishop have authority over the professors. The rector also is to be named by his professors, who give no guarantee of their orthodoxy. The philo-slaves would be particularly satisfied if this rector were himself a layman; they would see without displeasure authority wholly taken away from the bishop and passed into the hands of the laity. I know that certain Protestant sects look at the matter thus; but I ask myself, how can men who think thus persuade themselves that they are orthodox? above all, how can they persuade others so? What shall we say? Are these philo-slaves a sect which the Russian Church will end by ejecting from its bosom, or rather is it necessary to explain this phenomenon by the state of disregard into which the Russian clergy have fallen? We do not know; but this anti-clerical fanaticism of the philo-slaves most certainly affords much to think about.

The reflections contained in the anonymous work on *The White and Black Clergy* are quite as curious. The author finds that the education given in the Russian seminaries was already too Catholic, and that the *new regulation* is about to render it Jesuitical. Let us first see in what it was too Catholic. According to our anonymous writer, the seminary superiors were wrong to busy themselves about the goings-out of their pupils, and the relations these might have with the outside world, to look with an evil eye on those who frequented balls and theatres, and he thinks that generally they were kept at too great a distance from women. And yet he speaks of a professor who, in a seminary, gave a course of lessons to which ladies were admitted; he farther recognises that all the surveillance of superiors does not prevent the seminarists going to theatres, balls, &c. His great argument is, that all the seminarists ought some day to be married. First of all, if it is probable that the majority will marry, it cannot be said of any that he ought to be married; and even admitting that they all marry, is this a reason for not preserving their youth from the wanderings and disorders to which they are too exposed? The vigilance — very insufficient, alas! — adopted by the seminary superiors to protect the innocence of their pupils, this is what our anonymous author speaks of as *Catholic tendencies!* What an avowal, what homage ! He would doubtless see this Catholic spirit replaced by tendencies wholly opposite—*orthodox* tendencies. Whither these would tend can be imagined. Once more, we are not the advocates of the Russian Church; but we do not believe that she deserves the opprobrium of being defended after this fashion.

As to the *Jesuitical tendencies* of the new regulation, the occasion for such an accusation is this. The central administration communicated to the bishops a description of the little seminary of Paris, and from it were borrowed several arrangements in use there. Every one knows that the little seminary of Paris is not a college of Jesuits, that it is directed by secular priests, under the supervision of the archbishop; but at this distance one may not look at this matter with minuteness, and two pages farther on our anonymous author does not hesitate to say, in reference to the Léotade affair, that among the *Brothers of the Christian Schools*—at Toulouse—*all, even to the servants and the physician, were Jesuits.* But in what, then, do these *Jesuitical tendencies* consist ? There are, firstly, the same grievances we have already seen in the organ of the philo-slaves : the seminaries are placed under the authority of the diocesan bishop; the rector, on his side, has too great a power in the house, the lay element

in the *personnel* is weak. Then come other
accusations of the same kind : instead of day-
schools the seminaries are going to become
boarding-schools; the pupils are separated too
much from the world ; Catholic seminaries are
taken as models, instead of imitating the Protestant system; mention is not often enough
made of the necessity of inculcating in the
youths devotion to their fatherland and to
the emperor. In other terms, the aspirants to
the priesthood ought to be accustomed to the
thought that they are, above all, functionaries of
the state. But what is more Jesuitical is, that
the bishop shall choose from his clergy an educated and pious priest charged to receive the confessions of the seminarists; this chaplain is recommended to excite in his penitents a sincere
contrition, to see them from time to time, to
give them good counsel, to habituate them to
watch over their actions and thoughts, to seek
their spiritual father in order to disclose to
him the state of their souls, to learn from him
to fight against their faults, and to exercise
themselves in mental prayer. The first objection our anonymous friend makes to this is not
without originality : a priest capable of discharging these functions is not to be found;
those of the monks who would be able occupy
more important posts; and to find one of them

in the ranks of the secular clergy too high a
salary would be necessary. And then this
would considerably alter custom. To-day the
seminarists are thought to confess and communicate twice a year, during the first week of
Lent and during Holy Week. In reality they
generally confine themselves to approaching the
sacraments at the beginning of Lent. Almost
all go to pass Easter in their families; starting
on Palm Sunday, because, from the bad state of
the roads, they do not reach home till Monday
or Tuesday. Scarcely any one approaches the
sacraments, which, however, does not hinder
the curés from giving them on their return a
certificate attesting that they have both confessed and communicated.* The *new regulation* prescribes two communions more per year,
the one at Christmas, the other at the Assump-
tion; as this latter festival falls during the
vacation, it may be feared that many young
men do not refrain from bringing a false
certificate. It also ordains that, in order to
give the seminarists habits of piety, prayers
should be recited morning and evening, grace
before and after meat should be said, and their
classes be begun and finished with a short

---

* In several Jesuit colleges there are vacations at Easter, but
the pupils leave only the day after the festival. This is a *Jesuitical*
invention which the Russian seminaries would do well to adopt.

prayer. And herein consists its Jesuitical tendencies. The seminarists receive a too clerical education, and the clergy are too isolated from the rest of the population. The less the priests shall distinguish themselves from the laity, the better it will be: they are married and fathers of families; consequently the principle is laid down, it remains only to deduce therefrom its consequences. It is necessary that the aspirants to the priesthood should be brought up by laymen, and as laymen; that they should have the same ideas, the same habits, the same kind of life as laymen. The greater part of the laity do not conform to the laws of the Church, and do not lead Christian lives. It matters not.

But what, then, is the priest, and why did our Lord call him the salt of the earth? Has he not received the deposit of revealed truth, in order to dissipate ignorance and combat error? Ought he not to oppose the doctrine of the Gospel to the false wisdom of the world? Has he not been established guardian of the law and dispenser of the sacraments? Ought he not to reprove sinners, to call them to penitence, to purify them from their defilements, to catch them up when fainting, and raise them to God? In a word, ought he not to react against ignorance, against errors, against vanity, against the corruption of the world? It is not, then, whilst living the life of the world, accepting its ideas and submitting to its influence, that the priest will be able to fulfil his mission. And if the men who drew up the new regulation of the Russian seminaries have insisted on the necessity of sheltering the priest's youth from the scandals of the world, they have only conformed to the spirit of the Gospel. Let people say that these are Jesuitical tendencies, *we* shall not complain; they thereby only establish the conformity of the spirit of the Company of Jesus with the spirit of Him who said, ' If ye were of the world, the world would love you; but because ye are not of the world, because I have separated you from the world, therefore the world hates you.' (John xv. 19.)

Consequently, the principles of the new regulation are good, so far as we can judge of them from the criticisms they have evoked. Will there be found in the Russian Church men to put them in practice? This is another question. Have these principles always been applied with discretion? We will not affirm it.

It is certainly a good thing to give habits of piety to clerical youth; but in making all the pupils attend mass Wednesdays and Fridays, matins and vespers every Sunday and holiday; by rendering it obligatory on them during their four last years at the seminary to

attend mass, matins, and vespers every day—
has not the limit of moderation been passed?
We think so. If we consider that the Offices
of the Russian Church are much longer than
those of the Latin, we shall feel a difficulty in
understanding that study does not suffer therefrom; and farther, 'tis doubtful whether they
be a proper means for nourishing piety. When
our anonymous author says that these long
hours of service are more in place in a monastery than in a house for study, that they can
produce in young souls distaste for prayer, or
dispose them to hypocrisy, we perfectly agree
with him. We shall say as much of the four
annual communions. We would that the young
men could approach the sacraments far oftener;
but, as each of these communions is preceded
by an eight days' retreat, without studies, without recreation, without distraction of any sort,
we expect from them no good result. One retreat a year may do very much good; but one
is sufficient, and farther, for very young men,
eight days are too long. Moreover, children
must not be left to themselves; they need to
be spoken with four or five times a day, and
fresh food always supplied them for mind and
heart.

In a word, the new regulation bears witness
to good intentions; but we doubt much if it

will breed happy effects. To speak our mind
entirely, we do not believe in the possibility of
a reform of the Russian seminaries. The evil
is too deep, and the men are wanting.

In such a situation there is but one course
to take : to allow those who can do anything
to do it. Renounce frankly your traditional
policy in matters religious; break all the fet-
ters with which you have loaded alien worship;
allow Catholics and Starovères (dissenters) to
have their seminaries, their academies, their
faculties of theology, as you freely allow them
to Protestants; do not burden these establishments with your administrative guardianship,
leave the bishops free to organise their seminaries as they desire, to entrust the direction of
them to whom they will, give all the religious
orders—not excepting the Jesuits—the faculty
to have colleges; efface from your code the
laws which forbid Russians to embrace any
other religion than that of the State : this free
concurrence can alone save you. I willingly
admit that the official Church will see the number of her children diminish; but the multitude of those inscribed on the parish registers
do not constitute her strength, as the 40,000
Catholics she conquered in 1867 add nothing
to her vigour. This is certain, that this concurrence will strengthen the Christian element

in the empire; that it will be an embankment against the *Nihilism* now propagating itself through the schools, and above all, says the *Moscow Gazette*, through the schools of the clergy. All the regulations in the world can avail nothing, the remedy must be sought elsewhere; and you will find it only in a renunciation of all your traditions opposed to alien worship.

CHAPTER IV.

THE BISHOPS.

THE Church founded by Jesus Christ is apostolic; it was to the Apostles that our Lord confided the deposit of the faith, the mission to teach all nations, the power to administer the sacraments, the task to lead the faithful into the way of salvation. The Apostles were mortal; their ministry is to be exercised until the consummation of the ages. They must therefore have successors: these are the bishops. The bishops are doctors; that is to say, guardians, interpreters, and judges of doctrine. They have the fulness of the priesthood; not only do they administer the sacraments, but they confer the power to administer them. They are pastors; to them belongs the care of leading and feeding the flock of Jesus Christ. What the bishops have received from the Apostles they transmit to their successors; and thus is formed in the Church a chain, of which not a link is broken —an uninterrupted tradition by which, from generation to generation, pass the teaching, the episcopal character, and authority.

The bishop's power is supernatural; it comes not from men, nor can it. Neither the votes of the people assembled in their comitia, nor a sovereign's decree, whatever his power, can make a bishop. To the ancients, when being entrusted with the government of the churches founded by him, St. Paul said: 'The Holy Ghost has made you bishops, to rule the Church of God.' 'Tis necessary, however, that men intervene in this great work of the transmission of the episcopal power. The first bishops were directly named and consecrated by the Apostles: about this there could be no difficulty. We shall presently see how the mode of election has been regulated by the canon law at different epochs in history; but before quitting the Apostles we must make an important observation.

When they began to preach the Gospel, not being able, of course, to address themselves to all men at once, they betook themselves to the great centres of population — to Antioch, Ephesus, Corinth, Thessalonica. When they had grouped around them a certain number of believers, and had sufficiently instructed them, before leaving them they placed at the head of this nascent Church a bishop, charged to rule it, and to carry on the work begun. This bishop spread the Gospel in the surrounding

towns, and there formed churches, to which, in
his turn, he gave bishops. The new churches
considered themselves as the daughters of that
which had begotten them in the faith; they
regarded her as a mother, and the city where
she was established became for them a *mother-
city*, a metropolis; for such is the signification
of the word. This is the origin of the ties of
subordination which attach sees simply episcopal to sees metropolitan.

There exists no necessary bond between
provinces ecclesiastical and provinces of civil
administration; but nothing was more natural
than for the Church to adopt administrative
boundaries, based in general on the very nature
of things. It hence resulted that, generally,
the metropolitan see was fixed in the chief city
of the province. But these sees themselves
were too numerous not to feel the need of
grouping themselves around a common centre.
The prefecture of the East was divided into five
great circumscriptions, which bore the names
of the Egyptian, Eastern, Asian, Pontian, and
Thracian dioceses. Also we early see the bishops of Alexandria, Antioch, Ephesus, Cæsarea,
of Cappadocia, and of the Thracian Heraclea,
exercising a certain authority over the metropolitans of their jurisdiction. The title borne
by the titularies of these great sees was not

uniformly fixed at their origin. The bishops
of Ephesus, of Cæsarea, and of Heraclea, were
called *Exarchs* ; later, the name of *Patriarch* was given to those of Alexandria and
Antioch.

At the epoch of its foundation Constantinople depended on the see of Heraclea. The
importance of the Bishop of Byzantium increased
with that of the city, which had become the
capital of the empire, and the see of Constantinople soon ranged under its authority all the
metropolitans of the diocese of Thrace, as well
as those of the dioceses of Asia and of Pontus.*
Jerusalem was then a simple bishopric, having
for its metropolis Cæsarea in Palestine, itself
subject to the authority of Antioch. But Christians could not forget that in Jerusalem was
accomplished the mystery of our redemption :
the finding of the Cross by the Empress Helena,
the magnificent basilica built over the Holy
Sepulchre by order of Constantine, the con-
course of pilgrims,—everything contributed to
raise the importance of this Church. The bi-

* On the origin of the see of Constantinople, and the circumstances which added to its importance, see the remarkable work
of Dr. Hergenrœther, *Photius Patriarch von Constantinopel, sein
Leben, seine Schriften und das griechische Schisma*, Regensburg,
1867. The first book is devoted to the history of the see of Constantinople from its foundation to Photius. It is greatly to be
wished that this important work, written in German, should be
soon translated into other languages.

shop of the holy city could scarcely remain in the last rank of the hierarchy. Councils, the interpreters of the feelings of the faithful, detached from the jurisdiction of Antioch a certain number of dioceses, of which was formed the patriarchate of Jerusalem.* Alexandria and Antioch have remained invested with a supremacy recognised from all time. Thus were formed the four great patriarchates of the East,—Constantinople,† Alexandria, Antioch, and Jerusalem. The Bishop of Rome was patriarch of all the West.

Unity is the law of the Church. There was one sole bishop in each diocese; several bishops grouped themselves around one sole metropolitan; several metropolitans around one sole patriarch. The patriarchs, in their turn, must have a centre. Our Lord had given a head to the Apostolic College in the person of St. Peter. The bishops of Rome, successors of St. Peter, had remained invested with an authority extending over the Universal Church. This authority, perfectly recognised in the East, was invoked only in extraordinary circumstances;

---

* This may be said without prejudice of the blame merited by the ambitious intrigues of some bishops of Jerusalem. See *Photius*, by Dr. Hergenrœther, vol. i. book i.

† After Rome, the second place among patriarchates was not definitively recognised at the see of Constantinople till much later.

short of these it was enough to have recourse to the patriarchs.

Such was the ancient organisation of the hierarchy in the Church.

When the Russians embraced Christianity, the Patriarch of Constantinople sent them a bishop, who remained subject to his authority. The Christian faith having spread itself beyond the limits of Kieff, it soon became necessary to organise in Russia several dioceses; and the see of Kieff became metropolitan, without ceasing to be subordinate to the see of Constantinople. It is no part of our plan to give the history of the relations between the two Churches. We confine ourselves to saying that, subject in principle to Constantinople, in fact, the Russian Church very early found herself in possession of a certain autonomy. For a long period she was wholly governed by one single metropolitan, the Bishop of Kieff. It was then usual at that time to distinguish a metropolitan from a simple bishop. Later, when the Church of Ukraine separated itself from the Muscovite Church, each of them had at its head a metropolitan. That of Kieff exercised very extended rights in Ukraine and Lithuania; that of Moscow had the same authority in the north-east. Then also they knew how to distinguish ecclesiastical provinces.

At the close of the sixteenth century the patriarchate of Moscow was erected: four metropolitans were created under its jurisdiction. This number grew with time; and at length, in 1685, fifteen years before the death of the last patriarch, the old Church òf Kieff paled before her young sister of Moscow; the metropolitan of the Ukraine transferred to the Moscow patriarch the obedience he had always rendered to him of Constantinople. At the commencement of Peter I.'s reign, the Russian Church counted eight metropolitans. Not content with abolishing the patriarchate, the destroyer of the hierarchy suppressed the metropolitans also: in April 1724 not one remained. The last survivor, Sylvester of Smolensk, had been transferred to the see of Tver, and reduced to the rank of bishop. The clergy saw with pain this overthrow, especially in Ukraine, where they remembered the almost complete independence they had enjoyed under the suzerainty of Constantinople; but they did not attempt to resist.

When Peter I. established the Synod, the bishops found themselves all on a level before this assembly, in which centred all authority. If to-day some bear the title of bishop, others that of archbishop, a few that of metropolitan, these distinctions are purely honorary; they

M

constitute a difference of provision without establishing any bond of subordination. Still farther, by a discipline unknown to antiquity, the title is attached to the person rather than to the see. There certainly exists a usage by virtue of which the bishops of Moscow, Kieff, and Petersburg, are metropolitans; but we have seen bishops succeed to the see of Moscow with the title of archbishop, and not receive till later that of metropolitan. Such was the case with Mgr. Filaret. Very lately Mgr. Gregory Posnikoff, before being promoted to the see of Petersburg, held that of Kazan with the title of metropolitan, which did not pass to his successor. These titles are given in the clerical career as that of privy councillor is in the civil.

From this state of things it results that the idea of hierarchy is obscured and almost effaced from the mind. Yet it has not completely disappeared. We recollect that ecclesiastical history and canon law speak of *provincial* councils; which involves the notion of ecclesiastical *provinces*, and of bishops subordinated to a metropolitan. To revive the use of these councils and to reëstablish the provinces is being thought of. The proof of this is in a very remarkable article, published by the *Moscow Gazette*, October $\frac{15}{27}$, 1866, No. 216.

Here is a passage, translated from the Russian:

'We must not, however, despise the danger the Orthodox Church runs through the outward disunion in which she now is. The Orthodox Church is essentially œcumenical, and it ought to appear in the character essential to it. The enemies of Russia, and the spirits hostile to œcumenical orthodoxy, who know it, seek to spread the opinion that the Russian Church has been completely transformed into a political institution; in consequence of which she finds herself, so far as a Church, in a state of inaction and death. *This is an exaggeration, but it must be confessed that such reports are not without a basis.* The œcumenical Church, in virtue of its constitution, ought to live the same life and to have the same spirit in every country on earth. In order to maintain œcumenical unity every Church ought to be found in living communion with all others; and the first condition for this, doubtless, consists in the living communion which each particular Church of the one œcumenical Church ought to maintain in its own limits (among its different parts), and for the preservation of which the canons of the Church have instituted the local or provincial councils. Anciently the provincial councils assembled twice a year under the presidency of the metropolitan; later, because of certain difficulties, the sixth œcumenical council permitted them to assemble only once a year in virtue of canonical laws which have not been abrogated by any legitimate authority. The provincial council, according to the canons of œcumenical councils, ought to be convoked by the circular letters of the metropolitan; it is this council which decides controverted ecclesiastical questions and doubtful cases; which examines complaints made against the bishops, which chooses them, institutes them, and judges them. Of these councils, established by the Apostles themselves (37th Apostolical Canon) we have had none for a long period. The Holy Synod cannot take their place, because all the bishops do not take part in its deliberations; whilst all the bishops ought absolutely to sit in the provincial councils, such as they were instituted by the Apostles and the councils œcumenical. Only old age, sickness, or some extreme necessity could excuse the bishop who did not every year present himself in the assembly of his brethren; otherwise he was subject to an ecclesiastical punishment. (Can. 87 of the Council of Carthage, 19th of the 4th Œcumenical Council, 50th of the 6th Œcumenical Council.)

Yet with us quite recently the diocesan bishops had still no right to go out of the limits of their dioceses for even the shortest time. This isolation of the bishops, contrary to apostolical constitutions and to the canons of the œcumenical councils, has had the most painful results for the life of the Church. It is but lately that our bishops have been permitted to absent themselves for eight days on notice being given to the Holy Synod, and for twenty-eight days with the previous authorisation of the Synod. Last summer, two bishops whose dioceses are contiguous to that of Moscow, Mgr. Irenarcus, Archbishop of Rezan, and Mgr. Antonius, Bishop of Smolensk, profited by this newly-acquired right. After doing reverence to the ancient sanctuaries of Moscow, they had in the Gethsemane Hermitage an interview with the metropolitan, Mgr. Filaret. These direct communications between the pastors of the Church cannot fail to send circulating through the body of the Church a sap new, living, and beneficent. The necessity of these interchanges of ideas daily makes itself more felt.

The present reign, whilst calling into new life the different elements of the national and political organisation, announces to the Church also the renewal of that life of which she was deprived, and the reëstablishment of the order of things bequeathed to us by the œcumenical councils. We have received news that the imperial defender of orthodoxy and the guardian of the Church's rights has invited the Holy Synod to deliberate on the reëstablishment of the canonical laws prescribing the convocation of councils, which, according to the apostolic decrees, should assemble every year. When councils shall have been reëstablished among us, their deliberations will put the bishops in direct relations with one another, and will introduce into the Church that life which formerly animated her; and then our Church will acquire the possibility of entering into relation with other orthodox Churches, and will become œcumenical no longer in name only, but also in fact. Then will the malevolent reproaches addressed to her by our secret and open enemies fall of themselves.'

We know not where those secret and public enemies of the Russian Church are which M. Katkoff, the editor of the *Moscow Gazette*, refers to. We are not afraid to assure him that all Catholics will applaud his language, and that no one wishes to see the accomplishment of the reforms in question more than we do; but we can speak only of that which exists, and even the article of the *Moscow Gazette* finds fault with an important omission. The eminent publicist cites the canons which attribute to the provincial councils the right of electing, judging, and deposing bishops. Let us see how these canons are observed in the Russian Church, and first let us take a glance at history.

The Apostles themselves appointed bishops in the Churches they founded; but the first disciples of the Apostles, such as Titus and Timotheus, perceiving no longer the same personal ascendency, chose bishops only with the concurrence of the faithful.* There were thenceforward, well says Dr. Hefele,† whom here we follow, two factors, which concur, each in its share, in the election. The Church, that is to say the faithful, brought its testimony in favour of the candidate; it declared him worthy (ἄξιος) of the episcopate,‡ and the disciple of the Apostles confirmed the election. When the immediate disciples of the Apostles had in their turn disappeared, the mode of electing was again modified. The clergy and the people of the Church to be provided for proposed a candidate, and the bishops of the province immediately instituted and ordained the elected. Sometimes the people did not present sufficient guarantees, or made a bad choice. Then the bishops directly proceeded to the election, in which, in the two cases, they had always the principal share.§ The Council of Nicæa deemed

---

* Συνευδοκησάσης τῆς ἐκκλησίας πάσης. S. Clem., 1st Epist. to the Corinthians, xliv.

† Hefele (C. J.), now Bishop of Rottemburg, *Concilien Geschichte*, vol. i. p. 366 et seq. ‡ 1 Tim. iii. 7.

§ Hefele, op. cit. vol. i. p. 367. He cites Cyprian, epist. 68— Beveridge, Συνόδικον, seu *Pandectæ Canonum* (Oxonii, 1672), vol.

it necessary to more clearly determine the powers of the electing bishops. It willed that at least three bishops, carrying the written consent of the other bishops of the province, should take part in the election, which must afterwards be confirmed by the metropolitan. (Conc. Nic. can. 4.)*

In the Latin Church the discipline has varied with the times. The right to elect has been often conferred on chapters; a great number of concordats have ceded it to the sovereign, substituted for the people, who exercised the same right in the primitive Church. For some time past there has been observed in different Churches a progressive return to the ancient custom of having the bishop elected by the bishops of the same province, or by the provincial council. In certain cases the mode of election partakes of different systems; but the confirmation, or institution, is always reserved to the Pope. To speak properly, the chapters, bishops, and princes here play the same part as the people in the ancient elections; the definitive election, formerly exercised by the metro-

---

ii. app. p. 47—Van Espen, *Commentar. in Canon. et Decret.* (Colon. 1755), p. i. tit. xiii. no. 10.

* The question here is both of the election and of the consecration of the bishop. The same principles are found in the Councils of Antioch, in 341, can. 19; of Laodicea, between 343 and 381, can. 12; the second c. of Nicæa, in 787, can. 3.

politan with the assistance of the bishops, is transferred to the Holy See. St. Cyprian, in the passage (Epis. 68) indicated above, distinguished the *suffragium* and the *judicium;* he attributed the suffragium to the whole of the clergy and people, whom he named *fraternitas,* the *judicium* remaining the apanage of the bishops. To-day the *suffragium* belongs to the *fraternitas* represented whether by the chapter, the prince, or by the bishops, and the *judicium* is reserved to the Apostolic See.

In the United Oriental Churches the *judicium* belongs to the patriarch, without reference to Rome. Only the patriarch himself asks of the Pope his own confirmation; but he is elected by the bishops of his nation, and begins to exercise his jurisdiction from the very day of his election.

In all the Churches separated from Rome there is the same discipline. Everywhere the patriarch, or he who fills his place, confirms the nominated bishops when he does not nominate them himself. If the fiction be admitted in virtue of which the Synod represents the patriarch, it is quite natural that the *judicium* should belong to him. The time to treat of the Synod is not yet come; but we are of M. Katkoff's opinion, that there would be every advantage in the *suffragium* being exercised by the bishops of the province, and even in leaving the *judicium* to the Synod there would be great improvement; for it is obvious that, except for grave reasons, the Synod should always confirm the choice of the bishops.

This is the place to recall another important disposition of the canonical law. When we study the history of the Greek Church we readily perceive that the councils, having before their eyes too frequent proofs of all the inconveniences inherent in the interference of the Byzantine emperors in the choice of bishops, endeavoured to prevent a return to it by granting to the bishops the right of election. These councils speak not of a pretended election, but of a true election, in which every one is free to vote for him whom he judges to be worthy of the episcopate. This is why the 3d canon of the second Council of Nicæa (787) agreeing on this point with the 31st apostolical canon, *declares null the election of a bishop when it has been made by the prince.* The reason of it is very simple : the emperors could not give to the bishops a jurisdiction *which they themselves did not possess.* Farther, it was necessary to prevent the favour of the eunuchs from placing in the chair of Chrysostom and Athanasius, as was too often seen, an Arian, Nestorian, Monophysite, or Iconoclastic priest. The Church ought to reserve to itself the right of driving away men disguised as pastors, who would have been only mercenaries, courtiers, perhaps wolves.

It might be admitted up to a certain point that the Russian bishops could be designated by the emperor, provided that the Synod were invested with sufficient authority armed with independence enough never to sanction an unworthy choice, and one which conscience disapproved. Is this exactly the case? And if the intervention of the Synod is only a fiction, a formality, must it not be concluded therefrom that the third canon of the second Council of Nicæa nullifies all episcopal nominations? And have not the *Staroveres* (dissenters) serious motives for refusing their obedience to bishops whose nominations are not canonical? Let them ridicule as they will those rude peasants transformed into bishops by the imposition of the hands of the metropolitan of *Béla Krinitza** (White Fountain), the canon of the council does not reach them; they at least do not hold their commission from the tsar.

Lately, moreover, the Synod of St. Petersburg, consulted by the Patriarch of Constantinople on the affairs of the Roumanian Church,

---

* See on this subject Eckardt, *Modern Russia* (London, 1870), in the chapter 'The Greek Orthodox Church of Russia and her Sects.' (*Trans.*)

recommended to the Roumanian bishops, in reference to the innovation attempted by Prince Couza, to place themselves in presence of the 30th apostolic canon and to examine their consciences. What says this canon? 'If any bishop, making use of the secular power, thereby obtain a Church, let him be deposed and separated, and all who communicate with him.'*

We put it to any candid man, is it impossible to find in the Synod's communion a bishop indebted for his elevation to the secular powers? It would, on the contrary, be very difficult to find one not touched by this canon. But let us confine ourselves for the moment to establishing that there has been at least one bishop incontestably smitten by the 30th apostolic canon —Theophane Prokopovich. This man, at first a United Greek, after having studied at Rome, came to seek his fortune in Russia. Not only did he strip himself of his Catholicism as an obstacle to his career, but farther adopted doc-

* This canon, cited as the 30th by the Synod, bears the no. 31 in the collection of Dionysius Exiguus, and no. 29 in that of Hardouin, Mansi, &c. See Hefele, *Concilien Geschichte*, app. at the end of vol. i. The very text of this canon sufficiently proves that it is not of apostolic origin. From the time of the Apostles, it could not be supposed that any bishop had obtained a bishopric by the favour of Nero or of his ministers; but the tenor of the canon must have been borrowed from some ancient council of the time of the Christian emperors. In any case, the Oriental Church, and the Russian Church with her, fully admits the authority and authenticity of this canon.

trines wholly Protestant. He made his way
rapidly, despite his unorthodox opinions, which
marked him out for the animadversion of the
Russian bishops. Peter I., charmed with his
docility, and wishing to make him the instrument of the reforms he was meditating, resolved
on raising him to the episcopate. Stephen Yavorski was then governing the Russian Church
as the patriarch's vicar. This man forwarded
to the tsar a memorial for preventing this pro-
motion, alleging the doctrines of the candidate,
and grounded his opinion on twelve extracts
taken from a thoroughly Protestant book written by Prokopovich under this title, *The In-
supportable Yoke.** Yavorski demanded that at
least Theophane should retract his errors. Peter
himself questioned the accused, found his explanations satisfactory, passed on and had him
consecrated Bishop of Pskoff, June 1st, 1717.
(*Russian Talk*, 1860, vol. i. p. 101.)†

If Theophane Prokopovich fall not under
the ban of the apostolic canon, we truly know
not to whom to apply it; and if he cannot escape this censure he is excommunicated, he and
all who have fellowship with him, that is the
Synod and the whole *official Church.* The

---

* Объ игѣ неудобносимомъ. A Latin translation of this work
appeared in 1782 in Leipzig, under the title *De Jugo Intolerabili.*
   † русская бесѣда.

letter too which the Synod lately addressed to the Patriarch of Constantinople respecting the affairs of the Roumanian Church, and which we shall quote farther on, justifies the Staroveres, who are unwilling to accept the communion of the Synod.

M. Katkoff considers the reforms already made under the present reign as preliminary to others. We fully coincide with this view, whilst taking into account one observation. Among the causes which have contributed to awaken in minds the desire of seeing the Russian Church recover her autonomy and independence, it would be unjust to forget the establishment of the Starovere hierarchy.

These proscribed and despised people, after two centuries of persecutions and contempt, have appeared all at once with an episcopate at their head, without any governmental connection, without bureaucracy, without sacerdotal caste. 'Tis not only the persecution which has ceased; contempt and scorn have also had their day. People began to say, why should not we also be independent of the State? How to throw off the encroachments of bureaucracy? How put an end to the development of Leviteism? Let not the official Church forget it; she is receiving lessons from the Starovere Church; and if to-day the *Moscow Gazette* speaks to us of provincial councils, if this question become the subject of the Synod's deliberations, this whisper of independence, these first symptoms of awaking, it is to the Starovere Church, to her hierarchy in the Austrian Empire, to the Metropolis of Béla-Krinitza, that they are owing. Nor are we at the goal.

See to-day the philo-slaves extending their hands to the Staroveres. Ah! if these new recruits came to reinforce the ranks of those valiant athletes, we should rejoice at it. But we much fear there is a misunderstanding which will be powerful for evil to the *Staroveres*. Yes, the philo-slaves are *rascolniks* (sectaries). This is not difficult to see; but they will never accept any hierarchy; their place is not in the Starovere Church, not even in the ranks of the *Bezpopovstchina;** it is in the extreme sects which reject all authority.

Let us return to our subject. The bishops in Russia are named by the emperor: the Synod confines itself to countersigning the imperial nominations, and every one knows that it has not authority enough to enter into a struggle with power; its approval, then, is only an empty and insignificant formality.†

---

* безпоповщина (without priests). So are called a large portion of the Russian dissenters, subdivided into many sects, and admitting of no priest of any kind. (*Trans.*)

† According to a resolution of Peter the Great (Feb. 14, 1721),

The canons of the councils cited by M. Katkoff reserve to the provincial council the right of judging and condemning bishops. None can be deprived of his see except after sentence from this tribunal pronouncing his deposition. The Church has wished to guarantee their irremovability as a first condition of their independence. On this point, again, the canon law is not observed in Russia. We find at once the proof of this in the ease with which the bishops are transferred from one see to another. We shall perhaps be told that in the Catholic Church also translations are to-day not rare. We grant that the ancient discipline has on this point been relaxed, and even that translations have sometimes their advantages; but, at least in the Catholic Church, one rarely sees a bishop translated more than once, and never against his will; whilst it is quite otherwise in Russia. Mgr. Filaret, who, at his death in 1857, was Metropolitan of Kieff, had formerly been Bishop of Kalouga, Archbishop of Rezan, and Archbishop of Kazan. In 1863 died a bishop named Smaragdus, who had occupied in succession *seven* different sees. At one time for advancement, at another for disgrace, the

---

the Synod presents two names, the Emperor chooses one of them; but nothing is easier than to have inserted the one intended beforehand.

Russian bishops pass from one diocese to another with as much facility as elsewhere a préfet from a prefecture; and but very little heed is paid as to their consent.

'Tis not only by the aid of these indirect means that a blow is given to the principle of irremovability. Peter I. and his successors had never troubled themselves to depose bishops with whom they were discontented, though they had no canonical fault to reproach them for. Thus in 1718, Dositheus, Bishop of Rostoff, was degraded, put to the torture, and broken on the wheel; and when he had expired, his head, severed from the trunk, was fixed upon a pike, and his body delivered to the flames.

What, now, was his crime? The convent where Peter had shut up his own wife, that he might more freely satisfy his adulterous passions, was situated in Dositheus's diocese; the bishop was reproached with having allowed the tsarina to wear secular garments, and with having entertained her with visions and prophecies announcing the approaching death of the emperor.[*]

---

[*] Ustryaloff, Исторія Царствованія Петра Вешкаго (*History of the Reign of Peter the Great*), Спб. 1858, vol. vi. pp. 213, 219, 224, 226. русскій Вѣстникъ (*Russian Messenger*), June 1863, p. 463.—At the same epoch Joseph Krakowski, Archbishop of Kieff, was arrested and conducted under escort to Petersburg. This aged man of seventy succumbed on the road, and died at Tver. It was then

In 1721 Aaron, Bishop of Carelia, was shut up in a convent.* In 1725 Theodosius, Archbishop of Novgorod and vice-president of the Synod, was stript of his dignity and imprisoned.† In 1727 Philotheus of Tobolsk was obliged to retire into a monastery.‡

At the accession of the Empress Anne, when Biren became all-powerful, persecution again set in with redoubled rigour. Barlaam Vonatovicz, Metropolitan of Kieff, was degraded in 1730 (ukase, Nov. 30th) without any one's troubling himself to say why. It is said that he had omitted to chant the *Te Deum* on an imperial fête-day. According to other accounts, Prokopovich had a grudge against him for having had printed a fine edition of Etienne Yavorski's 'Stone of the Faith' (*Kamen very*). Leon Yourloff, Bishop of Voronége, was degraded at the same time as Barlaam Vonatovicz, and besides suffered the punishment of the knout in public.‖ Georges Dashkoff, Archbishop of Rostoff, and Ignatius Smola, Bishop

---

acknowledged that he was innocent of the fault alleged against him. Ibid. p. 255; note, *Justificatory Papers*, 175, 176, and 188.

* *Russian Messenger*, June 1863, p. 463, article by M. Melnikoff on the Staroverean Bishops.

† *Russian Messenger*, June 1863, p. 463. ‡ Ibid.

§ Filaret, Исторія русской Церкви (*History of the Russian Church*), tom. v. pp. 57, 68, 119 : see especially the notes.

‖ Filaret, op. cit. vol. v. pp. 58, 119; *Russian Messenger*, June 1863, p. 463.

of Kolomna,* members of the Synod, were both
stript of their dignity, in December 1730, for
not having shown *sufficient eagerness in condemning* the Bishop of Voronége, who was *innocent.*† Sylvester, Archbishop of Kazan, who
was noted for his zeal in propagating Christianity in his diocese, was degraded Dec. 31st,
1731.‡ Herodion of Tchernigoff was confined
in a monastery in 1734.§

Biren's most celebrated victim was Theophylact Lopatinski, Archbishop of Tver, and a
member of the Synod.

---

* Filaret, vol. v. pp. 58, 119, 120; *Russian Messenger*, June 1863,
p. 463.

† The true motive for the hatred conceived by Biren and Theophane Prokopovich against the Metropolitan of Kieff, the Archbishop of Tver, the Archbishop of Rostoff, the Bishop of Voronége,
and that of Kolomna, was the part these prelates had taken in the
negotiations opened at Moscow by the Abbé Jubé, delegate of the
Sorbonne, with the aid of the Duke of Liria, ambassador of Spain.
The object of these was the union of the Russian Church with the
Catholic. This happened in the reign of Peter II., and during the
ascendency of the Dolgoroukis. The idea of the reunion seems to
have had the support of Prince Basil Loukich Dolgorouky, afterwards executed, and that of several other members of his family.
The Abbé Jubé entered Russia as preceptor to the children of Prince
Sergius Dolgorouky, whose wife, the Princess Irene (*née* Galitzin),
had embraced Catholicism. These projects miscarried in consequence of the death of Peter II. and the accession of Anne, which
brought disgrace to the Dolgoroukies; and above all, by the Cal-
vinistic tyranny of Biren, seconded by hatred of Prokopovich and
of his worthy friend Prince Tcherkasky. It is remarkable that for
200 years past the saddest times in Russian history have been
those when anti-Catholic tendencies have had the upper hand.

‡ *Russian Messenger*, June 1863, p. 463; Filaret, vol. v. p. 119.

§ *Russian Messenger*, ibid.

We have already seen the opposition that Theophane Prokopovich met with in Etienne Yavorski. The vicar-patriarch was not content with wishing to impose on Theophane a retractation of his Protestant doctrines before his preferment to the episcopate; he had combated them in a great work entitled *The Stone of the Faith.* The credit of Prokopovich, and of the Protestants who surrounded Peter I., prevented this book from appearing; but in 1728, after the death of the tsar, Lopatinski, not content with having it printed, published also an apology for it. All the hatred Prokopovich bore Yavorski he devoted, after the death of the latter, to his disciple; on him he wreaked all his vengeance. He denounced the two works to Biren. All the copies were seized. Lopatinski, excluded from the Synod in 1730, cited in 1732 before the tribunal of the secret chancery, was beaten with rods, put to the torture, kept three years in solitary confinement, and after this stript of the archiepiscopal dignity and of the monastic habit, without the Synod's being called on to pronounce sentence;* then shut up in a fortress, where, smitten with paralysis, he languished until the accession of Elizabeth, who reinstated him in his dignity. And all this for having opposed the in-

* Filaret, op. cit. vol. v. p. 59, no. 101.

road of Protestantism into the Russian Church!
Other bishops, as we have seen, were ill-treated
for the same reason.　In 1736 Dositheus, Bishop of Koursk and Belgorod, was degraded.
In 1738 Hilarion of Tchernigoff and Barlaam*
of Pskoff were relegated to monasteries.†　In
1742 the same fate befell Peter of Belgorod
and Leonides of Kroutitsy.‡　It was, however,
by the devout Elizabeth that in 1748 Gabriel
of Oustioug was treated in the same manner;§
and in 1757 that Gennadius of Kostroma was
stript of the episcopal dignity.‖　And in the
liberal and enlightened reign of the great Catherine, Arsenius Matseievich, Archbishop of
Rostoff, having protested against the confiscation of the goods of the clergy, was stript of
his dignity, ranked as a layman, and shut up
in a fortress, where he died.　Arsenius belonged to the same school as Lopatinski; like
him he had written against the Protestants.

　　Can it, after this, be said that the Russian
bishops find in the organisation of the Russian
Church any guarantee whatever against despotism, or ought we to wonder at their becoming mute and losing even the last vestige of
independence ?

---

* *Russian Messenger*, June 1863, p. 463; Filaret, p. 120.

† Idem, ibidem.

‡ Id. ibid.　　　　　§ Id. ibid.　　　　　‖ Ibid.

Let us not be deceived; in our day forms have changed, but as little, or perhaps less, embarrassment is felt. The idea of an irremovable bishop, who could leave his diocese only for reasons of extraordinary gravity and after a judgment strictly and exclusively canonical, is an idea that occurs to the mind of no one. Nothing is more common than to read in the journals that such or such a bishop has been allowed a *repose*, and that for a residence such or such a monastery has been assigned him. This euphemism scarcely disguises a real deposition, much less an exile and a sort of prison.* Let a bishop wink at too crying abuses, or for any cause whatever draw on himself the dissatisfaction of the administration, he is *admis a se reposer*. Often he is ignorant of the cause of his disgrace, is cited before no tribunal, is not called on to defend himself, to produce witnesses, to prove his innocence, to invoke the prescriptions of the law. He has no other course to take than that of submitting to his fate.

We shall be told that these measures are taken under the guarantee and sanction of the Synod. We shall speak by and by of this high

* The bishops *admis à se reposer* received in 1866 the right of quitting the diocese assigned them for residence, provided they had the authorisation of the diocesan bishop.

assembly. But M. Katkoff has already told us that it would not be possible to assimilate the Synod to a provincial council. Then whatever the tribunal, there is no judgment. Finally, we refer to the opinion of the bishops themselves. Do they believe in finding a guarantee in the intervention of the Synod? This ends the matter. Not a bishop thinks anything of the sort.

Would to God that a member of the Russian Episcopate had the courage to publish the true history of those two great victims, Theophylact Lopatinski and Arsenius Matseievich! This would be the best apology to give to the world on behalf of that body; but, at the same time, the best proof that it would not be possible for him to recover his independence by solely relying on an ecclesiastical authority beyond the reach of the civil power: a truth perfectly understood by the Staroveres, who had taken care to give themselves a head residing out of the empire. Herein they had no design to imitate the Catholics; the nature of things and good sense were their only guides. Let people declaim as they will against a foreign power, in it precisely consists the unique guarantee for episcopal independence.

How the Russian bishops are nominated and how deposed we have just seen; it remains for us to examine how they exercise their authority.

Until very recently no bishop could leave his diocese without permission from the Synod; so that it was impossible for two bishops to visit each other, still more so to hold an assembly. More recently they have been authorised to absent themselves for eight days without permission, each time, however, notifying the fact to the Synod.* There is, doubtless, an ecclesiastical law respecting the residence of bishops, but this law does not go so far as to interdict them all movement, and especially not absences prompted by the interests of their dioceses. Like all other canonical laws, this has for its end the peace, independence, and liberty of the Church, and 'tis revolting to see it transformed into an instrument of slavery.†

---

* See the Annual Report of the chief procurator of the Synod for the year 1866.

† In the *Nord* of Dec. 20th, 1866, we read as follows: ' Mgr. Wolonczewski, Catholic Bishop of Samogitia, is perfectly free to fulfil his pastoral duties within the limits of his diocese. He is subject in his diocesan circuits only to the general obligation, common to him and *all* Russians, of having a passport and a visa; he is farther obliged, like *all* bishops, to reside in his diocese, which he cannot quit without superior authorisation. We know not if this obligation of residence, so painful to the prelates of the court of Louis XIV., and so often eluded by them, seems peculiarly hard to Mgr. Wolonczewski, but it will be granted that there is nothing unreasonable in it.'

So speaks the *Nord*. It will be allowed that this jeering tone, in a matter so grave and sad, is singularly out of place, and does

We have seen that, according to the new regulation of the ecclesiastical schools, the superiors of seminaries can be named by the Synod on the presentation of the diocesan bishop.

All the journals have combined to denounce this simple measure as an exorbitant invasion of episcopal authority. To us it seems strange that the bishop should not enjoy full independence in the exercise of a right which ought to be inalienable. Herein we appeal to all the Bishops of France.

In the memoir which Pope Gregory XVI. of glorious memory transmitted from hand to hand to the Emperor Nicholas, December 13th, 1845, his Holiness cites: 'Among the laws and anti-Catholic regulations which the Holy See could not, and cannot, cease to denounce, is the decree of November 30th, 1840, concerning seminaries, by which these have practically been withdrawn from the episcopal jurisdiction and subjected to governmental, as well for regulation of doctrine as of discipline.

---

little to inspire great confidence in the reader. For this prohibition to the bishops going outside their dioceses, we refer the *Nord* to the *Moscow Gazette;* but we should be curious to know if, as the *Nord* seems to admit, the Russian bishops need a passport in order to visit their diocese. If Mgr. Wolonczewski could visit his diocese only with a visa of General Kaufmann, it is probable that he did not visit it at all, at least until this general was displaced. It must be avowed that the *Nord* has a rare talent for confirming news which it pretends to contradict.

'*Such regulations are only developments or corollaries of principles injurious to the rights and divine authority of the Church, already contained in the laws and ukases recorded among the documents of the allocution of July 22nd, 1842. It is clear, however, that here is a body of laws, whose effect is to forbid to the bishops the exercise of their sacred pastoral ministry, taking from them all jurisdiction over discipline, worship, liturgy, instruction, and the seminaries; taking from them, in a word, the government of their churches, and subjecting them to the consistories, to the ecclesiastical college, and finally to the ministry, in order to reduce them to be mere executors of the sovereign's commands.*

'*These are, then, laws in open opposition to Divine ordination, since according to Scripture,* "Spiritus Sanctus posuit Episcopos regere Ecclesiam Dei" (*the Holy Ghost hath set the bishops to rule the Church of God*). *These are laws subversive of ecclesiastical authority, of the hierarchy of the Catholic Church, in a word, of its whole constitution.*'[*]

In holding this firm and noble language, Gregory XVI. probably never dreamt that he

[*] *Esposizione documentata sulle costanti cure del S. P. Pio IX. a riparo dei mali che soffre la Chiesa Cattolica nei dominii di Russia e di Polonia,* Roma, 1866, pp. 4, 5. A French translation, with Introduction by the Oratorian Fath. Lescœur, appeared in Paris under the title *L'Eglise de Pologne:* V. Palmé, 1868.

was pleading the cause of the Russian bishops. 'Tis they, and not the Catholic bishops, who have profited thereby. We hope that they will be grateful to him, and understand that it is not useless to the Episcopate to have a head capable of taking up its defence, when the bishops cannot, or dare not, raise their voices.

These very judicious observations of Gregory XVI. apply not only to the seminaries; they extend to all the acts of episcopal administration. If we enter into detail, we shall always reach the same results. In Russia all authority is concentrated in the Synod; the bishop can do nothing of himself; his life is passed in sending reports to Petersburg, receiving thence orders, executing them, and notifying his obedience. Instead of having, as in France, a council composed of priests of his choice, the Russian bishop is assisted by a consistory in which sit priests, 'tis true, but where figures also a lay secretary nominated at Petersburg by the Synod on the presentation of its chief procurator, but in reality named by him. The secretary takes cognisance of all business, draws up all documents, and conducts all correspondence. He is assisted by a chancery, composed of six or seven chief clerks, with their sub-clerks and writers. To this chancery are

referred all the affairs of the clergy to the most
minute detail; and it is notorious that no business is transacted without drink-money. Russian bureaucracy has, in general, a sad reputation for venality; the bureaucracy of the consistories is more venal than any other. It is a true
system of drainage perfectly organised, which
draws off from priests, deacons, and poor clerks,
all their savings; a hideous plague which feeds
on the Russian clergy, whose revenues would
suffice them if delivered from these ignoble
spoliations.

Nothing is sadder than this bureaucratic
régime which strips the bishops of all authority, and makes them the victims of endless
annoyance; and all this in order to procure a
livelihood for the *wasters* of the seminaries, reduced to create for themselves a revenue by
their rapine. The creation of ecclesiastical
chanceries in all the towns of the arrondisse-
ment has been resolved on: its inutility, however, is so perfectly demonstrated, that, last
year, the part of the building in the chancery's
use having become a prey to fire, the chancery
was simply suppressed. The employés begged
to be allowed to rebuild the burnt house *at
their own expense;* so much interest had they
in not losing this engine for draining the
people. Thus, in whatever point of view we

look at the Russian Church, we see the plague of Leviteism.

In law authority belongs to the bishops; in the consistory everything is to be decided by the priests. But in practice 'tis the chancery or its chief, the secretary, who decides everything. It can scarcely be otherwise. In the course of a year from 12,000 to 15,000 files of papers pass the consistory, each claiming a decision according to law. Now the laws ecclesiastical, the statutes of the Synod, the decrees of the bishops, form an enormous mass of documents all unedited; a veritable chaos, where only men hoary in the business escape being lost. Let a member of the consistory feel inclined to decide otherwise than the chancery, he is plied with legal texts, and obliged to sign. The bishop himself is in no condition to strive with the secretary. Named by the chief procurator of the Synod, who alone can change him, the secretary is in direct correspondence with him, and renders him an account of the progress of business; it depends, then, on the secretary to forewarn the all-powerful chief procurator against the bishop. With still greater reason are the members of the consistory obliged to bend to him. The bishop does not attend their sittings; the secretary brings him the papers, and presents him with

a report; as the ordinary intermediary between
the bishop and the consistory, he can by means
of the bishop modify the decisions taken in the
assembly, or even, in transmitting to the latter
the orders of the bishop, give them the colour
that suits him. Almost always the only motive for the secretary's opinions is the money
he has received from interested parties.* One
word on the incomes of the bishops. In 1866
the *Moscow Gazette,* wishing to show that the
revenues of the Catholic bishops in Russia

* At the conclusion of the Concordat of Aug. 3d, 1847, which
was abrogated by a ukase of Dec. 4th, 1866, the plenipotentiaries
of the two parties did not succeed in coming to an understanding
on a certain number of points. These were embraced in a protocol,
signed the same day by Cardinal Lambruschini, Count Bloudoff,
and M. Bouteneff. This protocol was published at Rome in the
volume of documents relating to the Allocution of Oct. 29th, 1866
(*Esposizione documentata,* &c.). We deem it our duty to reproduce
article ii.

' *The pontifical plenipotentiary protested against the presence
in the episcopal consistories of a lay secretary named by the government, and uniting also the quality of imperial procurator. The
plenipotentiaries of his imperial majesty replied, that the imperial
government would be ready to submit the nomination of the secretary of the consistory to the previous consent of the bishop, reserving to itself in this case to establish a procurator at the consistory;
or else the imperial government would reserve to itself the nomination of the secretary without the participation of the bishop, in
this case renouncing the appointment of a special procurator.*

' *The pontifical plenipotentiary declared that none of these modes
could be admitted by the Holy See.*' (*Esposizione,* &c. p. 19.)

After the example of what has been done for the seminaries,
this remonstrance of the Holy See, rejected in the case of Catholic
bishops, could it not be admitted in favour of bishops of the
dominant Church ? The suppression of the lay secretary would

were higher than those of the bishops of the
National Church, published information which
we eagerly borrow from it.

'The Catholic Archbishop of Mohileff, resident at
Petersburg, receives from the Treasury a provision of
1383*l.*; that of the other Catholic bishops is from 800*l.*
to 1000*l.* On the other hand, the Metropolitan of Petersburg and Novgorod touches 5414r. 14k. (902*l.*); that of
Kieff, 4900r. (816*l.*); that of Moscow, 1712r. 16k. (285*l.*)
[How came M. Katkoff to quote this figure? Who proves
too much, proves nothing]; the Archbishops of Riga,
Tauris, Stavropol, Lithuania, Mohileff, Minsk, and Podolia, each 4000r. (666*l.*); those of Polotzk and Volhynia, 3200r. (533*l.*); the Archbishop of Cherson, 2414r.
85k. (402*l.*) the Bishop of Gouria and Abkhasia, 1500r.
(250*l.*); twelve Archbishops occupying important sees, as
those of Kazan, Astrakan, Tver, Rezan, 914r. 85k. (152*l.*);
and finally, twenty-six bishops, 743r. 40k. (124*l.*). Some
auxiliary bishops, as he of Moscow, touch only 358r. 98k.
(60*l.*); that is, less than many simple Catholic priests.

It may be said that the orthodox bishops receive something additional. These additions are not given for their
personal use; but for the maintenance of their cathedrals,
and of the *personnel* forming the episcopal house. Nor
are these additions considerable, 2000 or 3000 roubles.

---

result in the destruction of bureaucracy in the ecclesiastical administration. It would be not only the bishops, but the whole
clergy, who would celebrate this reform with thanksgiving and
extraordinary rejoicings ; see also (p. 145 of the same work) a
discussion on this point in a committee composed of Counts Nessel-
rode, Kisséleff, Bloudoff, and MM. Lanskoi, Turkull, Bouteneff,
Romuald Hubé, and Nicolas Kisséleff. In 1856 it was scarcely
possible to find names that would give more guarantees for justice
and impartiality ; but bureaucratic routine was still too strong.
Let us hope an advance has been made since.

Now every cathedral ought to have at least ten priests and deacons, who, having no parishes, receive a provision of 250r. or 300r. each (42*l.*-50*l.*). Some orthodox bishops derive revenues also from the immovables belonging to the bishopric, and receive gifts from the faithful; but these not being a charge on the Treasury, but voluntary offerings, cannot be taken into account.' (*Moscow Gazette*, Nov. 11th (23d), 1866, No. 238.)

If we verify these data by those furnished by the oft-cited work on *The White and Black Clergy*, the result is not quite the same. True, the *Moscow Gazette* has told us that the Latin Catholic Archbishop of Mohileff receives a provision of 8000 roubles, or 1333*l.*; but it has not told us that the Russian Archbishop of Varsovia receives as much. Now the diocese of Mohileff, which comprehends within its circumference both Petersburg and Moscow, is perhaps the vastest diocese of the Catholic Church, whilst the flock of the Archbishop of Varsovia in 1865 did not amount to 30,000 souls. The Archbishop of Riga, according to our author, does not receive 4000 roubles, or 666*l.*, as asserted by the *Moscow Gazette*, but 6700 roubles, or 1116*l.* The provision for the Archbishops of Lithuania, Mohileff, Minsk, and Podolia is quite 4000 roubles, or 666*l.*; but they have a supplement of 2973 roubles, or 495*l.*, making a total of more than 1000*l.* The Archbishops of Polotzk and Volhynia, besides their provision of 3200 roubles, or 533*l.*, receive a supplement of 2778 roubles, or 463*l.*, which secures to them a revenue of nearly 960*l.* The other bishops have also severally received supplements :

The Bishop of Irkoutsk	. . .	2000 R. =	£333
„	Olonetz . . .	2000 R. =	333
„	Kicheneff . . .	1530 R. =	255
„	Kalouga . . .	1428 R. =	236
„	Kostroma . . .	1142 R. =	190
„	Penza	1142 R. =	190
„	Kharkoff . . .	1000 R. =	166
„	Kherson . . .	857 R. =	143

The bishop of Stavropol has ceded to the state a mill and fisheries, and in return receives an annual rent of 3800 roubles, or 633*l.*, which, added to his provision of 4000 roubles, makes up a revenue of more than 1200*l.* Many bishops live in the enjoyment of fisheries, mills, meadows, and lands, which bring them more or less money. The emancipation of 1861 had the effect of securing to them, as a compensation for peasants attached to their service, a very liberally calculated indemnity. Besides, many bishops are at the same time abbots or superiors of monasteries whose revenues they deal with.

It was formerly the privilege of the three Metropolitans of Moscow, Kieff, and Peters-

burg, who are at the same time necessarily archimandrites of the three *laures* of St. Sergius,
of the Crypts, and of Nevsky. Little by little
other prelates also received convents *in commendam;* in 1842 there were eighteen com-
mendatories; in 1858, thirty-eight; in 1861,
forty-five. Some have even many convents;
and some of these are very rich. Thus, the
Metropolitan of Moscow, with a ridiculous provision of 1712 roubles, or 285*l.*, enjoys a revenue of more than 100,000 francs, or 4000*l.*

The Synod possesses a capital of 254,543
roubles, that is, more than 42,757*l.*, the income
of which is distributed among the bishops under
the name of supply. It is a custom with rich
families to call the diocesan bishop to burials;
each of these ceremonies brings him in one or
two hundred roubles, *i.e.* 16*l.* or 32*l.*, sometimes more. When the bishop goes to consecrate a new church, he receives an indemnity
which sometimes rises to 40*l.* or 80*l.* The bishops have domestic chapels, where collections
are made. In one of these chapels they collect
in a year 14,000 roubles, or 2333*l.* Miraculous
images are another source of revenue; sometimes abundantly so. We say nothing of illicit
and abusive profits. Provision, supplements,
indemnities, supplies accorded by the Synod,
monastic revenues, casualties,—all these suffice

to reassure us as to the pretended poverty of
the Russian bishops. They would certainly
not exchange their revenues for those of the
Catholic bishops, who receive on an average a
provision of 5000 to 6000 roubles, or 800*l.* to
1000*l.*, according to the *Moscow Gazette.**

If we pass to the moral authority, to the
influence of the bishops, we shall not be wrong
in affirming that it is almost *nil.* As to pastoral letters, they are never heard of. The dis-
courses they pronounce on solemn occasions
no one cares about. They can be haughty in
presence of their clergy, can surround themselves with a certain pomp, demand of their
inferiors excessive marks of respect, and, alas,
are no bolder or more independent in the presence of the great. They know not how to
unite Christian humility with sacerdotal firmness; people never hear them speak with an
evangelic liberty. Their action on minds, on
society, is *nil.* They seem to be bishops only
for the purpose of figuring in the pomps of the
divine office. The ceremonies of worship in
the oriental rite have, it is true, an incompar-
able majesty; in the Russian Church they are

* It would certainly be simpler to give the Russian bishops a
larger provision and suppress all these supplements, indemnities,
supplies, convents *in commendam.* But these are so many bonds
holding them in dependence on power. It is easier to suppress a
supplement than to diminish the provision.

performed with a rare perfection. The voice
of chanters lends them a marvellous charm,
and all this, as a whole, acquires completeness
only by the presidency of the bishop. This is
great; this is fine. But these splendours would
make no less impression, if the bishop, on lay-
ing aside his magnificent ornaments, remained
a bishop still; if he knew how to raise his
voice to instruct the people, to denounce abuses,
and to defend God's rights on earth and those
of the Church, of justice, of the humble and
lowly.

We will say of the bishops what we have
said of the priests and monks: it is not the
men that must be taken in hand, but the institutions. We have in our hands the Memoirs,
by M. Yakovleff, of the bishops who made part
of the Synod of his time; but although Yakovleff occupied the important post of chief procurator of the Synod, and had it in his power
to be well informed, it is repugnant to us to
cite him. Let us rather say that, in the condition made for them, there are to be met with
among the Russian bishops men distinguished
by the integrity of their manners, the gravity
and austerity of their lives, and by their disinterestedness. Who knows what that day will
bring forth when a crushing yoke shall cease
to rest on the Russian Church? If there is a

germ of health, 'tis in the episcopate. It is sometimes spoken of as a bough in which a little sap is left, and which is destined again to clothe itself with foliage.

The Russian bishops have the episcopal character, and if it has not always been legitimately transmitted to them, its validity has never been in doubt. We do not believe we shall do amiss by calling their attention to what is wanting to them—viz. independence. As bishops, they do not exercise in their plenitude their imprescriptible rights. They must allow us to say, they are not truly *bishops*, but *mitred functionaries*.

If the projects announced by M. Katkoff are realised, all hopes are justifiable. Yes, with that eminent publicist, we believe that if the ecclesiastical provinces were reëstablished, if provincial councils assembled and deliberated freely, if they chose bishops who should be irremovable and amenable only to their peers, if the ancient discipline were renewed —yes, we will hope it,—life could reënter this great body, numbed with centuries of lethargic sleep.

What consequences would a change so radical bring! M. Katkoff has perfectly sighted them. 'Tis not only the Russian Church which would be called to reconstitute itself; all the

Churches of the East must unite, as members long separated, to form a living body. From that moment provincial councils, presided over by a metropolitan, would no longer suffice; other councils, presided over by patriarchs, are needed; and rising higher still, an œcumenical council, representing the Universal Church. The œcumenical council must have also a chief, a president. Where is this chief of the hierarchy, around whom may gather respectfully the patriarchs themselves? The old Eastern Church knew him. 'Tis he who received the appeals of the patriarchs of Alexandria and Constantinople by the mouths of Athanasius and Chrysostom; he who deposed these same patriarchs in the persons of Nestorius, Anthemius, and Sergius;* who, by his legates, presided at the œcumenical councils: 'tis the Bishop of ancient Rome, 'tis the successor of St. Peter.

Let us pause. Our task is not finished; it remains for us to speak of the Synod.

* See the texts of the Russian liturgy which establish it, *Etudes*, 1st series, vol. ii. pp. 75, 76.

CHAPTER V.

THE SYNOD.

THE Russian Church, we have seen, was long
governed by a metropolitan dependent on the
Patriarch of Constantinople. The developments
of this Church, the increasing importance of
the country, the precarious situation of the see
of Constantinople after the capture of this city
by the Turks (1452),—all these considerations,
and many others, determined Boris Godounoff
to erect at Moscow a patriarchal see. Favoured
by circumstances, the new patriarch saw himself at first invested with very great authority;
but misunderstanding was not slow in cropping
up between him and the tsar. After a long
and painful strife, a council, convoked at Moscow by the care of the Tsar Alexis, and at
which the Eastern patriarchs assisted, deposed
the patriarch Nicon. He was replaced, and
nothing, externally at least, was changed in
the relations of the two powers. The patriarch's
authority, however, found itself diminished by
the struggle in which he had succumbed. At

first this was deemed to be only an eclipse; and had there arisen among Nicon's successors a man of intelligence and character, the lost ground had been recovered. Nothing of the kind occurred; but, on the other hand, a man was seen to mount the throne of the tsars endowed in the highest degree with those qualities which were essentially wanting in the chiefs of the Russian Church.

What at bottom were the religious ideas of Peter I.? This question is difficult and embarrassing. It is almost certain that he dreamt of a reconciliation with Rome,* but probably in view only of the matrimonial alliances which could be contracted with the houses of Austria and France. Besides sympathising with Protestants when very young, he was initiated into a masonic lodge founded at Moscow by Lefort. Hence it may be concluded that he was indifferent enough in matters of religion. He did not love the Russian clergy, the natural adversary of his reforms. Taught by the quarrels of his father Alexis with Nicon, and wishing to be master in everything and always, he resolved on abolishing the patriarchate, and replacing it by a council or college, to which

---

* See on this subject an interesting article of F. Gagarin, entitled *La Sorbonne de Paris et l'Eglise russe*, published in the *Etudes Religieuses*, &c. Sept. 1868. Paris.

he gave the name of Synod. This was a considerable innovation, which profoundly modified the hierarchy and the relations between the Church and the State, as well as the relations of the Russian Church with those of the East. It thus gave new strength to the schism of the Staroveres,—to that *raskol*, born indeed under his father, but to which, contrary to his intention, he communicated an extraordinary vitality.

Peter had to use caution; he felt it, and proceeded with a prudent slowness to the execution of his designs. The patriarch Joachim having died March 17th (27th), 1690, a few months after the revolution which deprived the Princess Sophia of power, the new tsar appointed as his successor Adrian, who showed himself but little favourable to his reforms, but otherwise caused him little embarrassment. At his death, in October 1700, Peter, without giving him a successor, confided the administration of the see to Stephen Yavorski, Metropolitan of Rezan. This provisional state lasted more than twenty years, and the sight of a patriarch in Russia had almost been forgotten, when the Synod was instituted, January 25th (o. s.), 1721.

An ecclesiastical statute, or regulation, determined the rights and duties of this assembly.

We have before us a Latin translation of it, printed at Petersburg in 1785, under the auspices of Prince Potemkin. 'Tis from it that we must learn the ideas of the tsar.

The regulation is composed of three parts. The first treats of the Synod and the motives for its foundation; the second, of the persons subject to its jurisdiction—viz. the bishops, schools, preachers, and laymen; the third, of the members of the Synod and their functions. Then come the rules imposed on the secular clergy, the monks, and nuns. It is a veritable ecclesiastical code, *still in force.*

The ukase is very remarkable. Peter congratulates himself on the happy reforms accomplished in the military and civil orders; he describes in general terms the disorders of the clergy, and the necessity of remedying them. Smitten with the fear of the Sovereign Judge, who will demand of him an account of the power intrusted to him, after the example of the kings of the Old and New Testaments, he undertook the reform of the ecclesiastical order. In pursuance of this he instituted a council or Synod, composed of a president, two vice-presidents, four councillors, and four assessors, to whose jurisdiction were assigned *all* the affairs of the Church of all the Russias, and whose judgment should be without appeal: so that everybody must acquiesce in the Synod's decrees and decisions, and rest satisfied with its definitive sentence. Moreover there is no mention made of the patriarchs, nor of the orthodox Church beyond the limits of the empire; no announcement that the tsar would at first put himself in accord with the Eastern Church, still less that he would admit the possibility of an appeal to the Church Œcumenical.

It was only eight months afterwards that Peter deemed it advisable to write to the Patriarch of Constantinople, informing him of what he had done, and inviting him to recognise the Synod, with which he would have the same relations as he formerly maintained with the Patriarch of Moscow. The patriarch Jeremy displayed little eagerness in replying, as is seen by his letter, dated September 23d, 1723, that is, two years after Peter wrote. Cuttingly contrasting with the usual forms of this kind of writing, it is short and dry. Jeremy confirms the Synod established by the most pious and most gracious autocrat, the sacred Tsar of all Muscovy. He declares that ' the holy and sacred Synod is, and is called, his brother in Jesus Christ, and that it has the power to do what the very holy and apostolical patriarchal sees do.' He exhorts it to preserve and keep steadily the customs and canons of the seven holy and sacred œcumenical councils, and all that the holy Eastern Church observes.

After the ukase comes the formula of oath. The members of the Synod swear to show themselves *faithful, upright, and obedient servants and subjects of the Autocrat of all the Russias; and after him of his legitimate heirs, designated or to be designated, in virtue of the good pleasure and sovereign power of his Majesty, as also of her Majesty the Tsarina Catherine.** They engage, as far as they shall be able, to preserve and defend all the rights and prerogatives belonging to the sovereignty, authority, and

---

* Peter had in 1689 married Eudoxia Lapoukhin, and by her had had two sons, of whom one, the Tsarovich Alexis, had himself left a son by his marriage with the Princess Charlotte of Brunswick. After having been married ten years Peter repudiated Eudoxia, and obliged her to retire into a convent, without giving any reason for his conduct. She survived Peter. Ecclesiastical authority never pronounced her divorce; besides, had it done so, the sentence must have been considered as extorted, since there existed no legitimate motive for breaking this union. This Catherine, to whom the members of the Synod took the oath of fidelity, and who eventually succeeded Peter I., could not then be the legitimate wife of the tsar; she was only his concubine. He had had three children by her when he declared her his wife (1711). Later, in 1724, he crowned her, but no authentic proof exists that the marriage was celebrated. There is no escape from this dilemma: either Peter married her during his lawful wife's life, and so committed bigamy, or he did not marry her; in any case, his connection with her was adulterous. Catherine could be in the eyes of the bishops, and really was, only a concubine. On seeing this cowardly complacence of the bishops in presence of adultery and bigamy, it is impossible not to think of Henry VIII., with whom Peter I. had more than one feature of resemblance.

power of his majesty, such as these rights and
prerogatives are defined, or shall hereafter be
defined, in their narrowest signification, without sparing their own lives; in watching in
all things for the advantage of his majesty; in
denouncing, hindering, and combating everything that could do him harm.   Finally, in
the formula of oath is found this significant
sentence: '*I confess and affirm on oath that the
sovereign judge of this Synod is the monarch of
all the Russias himself, our very clement lord.*'

Reserving the reflections which crowd on
us, let us continue our examination of the spiritual regulations.   In its first part Peter aims
at justifying the creation of the Synod.   He
invokes precedents, cites the Sanhedrim of the
Jews and the Areopagus of Athens; but, as
is seen, very little to the purpose.   He wishes
to rely also on the Word of God.   St. Paul has
said to the Corinthians, 'He is not the God
of confusion, but of peace. . . . Let all things
be done decently and in order' (1 Cor. xiv. 33;
40).   The tsar refers to these two texts; but
clearly perceiving that they are far from giving
formal sanction to his work, he refrains from
reproducing them.   Authorities failing him, he
tries argumentation.   Let us pass his argu-
ments in review.   1. Several men in association see more clearly into business than one

alone.   2. The decisions of an assembly carry
more authority than those of a single man.
3. The Synod will have so much more authority, as it shall be known that it is established
by the sovereign, and depends on him: *a
monarcha dependet, suamque illi acceptam fert
originem.* 4. Different occupations, sickness,
death, hinder a single man from dispatching
business, but do not impede an assembly.   5.
An individual is accessible to passion, interest,
corruption; not so an assembly.   6. A single
man yields more readily to the threats of the
powerful in the land.   7. The vulgar know
not the difference between the rights of princes
and those of the Church: when they see a pastor at the head of the Church, they are tempted
to compare him to the prince, and even to
place the spiritual order in the first rank. The
people could then be led to attach less importance to the orders of a monarch than to those
of a pontiff. With the Synod there would be
no such risk. Its president, deprived of all
prerogatives, stript of all pomp, can have no
high opinion of himself, and escapes the attempts of pride and flattery. The people,
knowing that this mode of government has
been established by order of the prince *man-
dato monarchæ*, will dwell in peace, being able
to count on no support from the spiritual au-

thority. 8. A patriarch could be judged only
by an œcumenical council, which would present many inconveniences; whilst each member of the Synod and the president himself are
amenable to the Synod.* 9. It is a method
of forming for the government of the dioceses
men destined to the episcopate, and the Synod
can be considered as a nursery for bishops.†

Such are the reasons which Peter I. deemed
proper to give to the public. We are tempted
to regard them as childish. At bottom there
are but two: the government of several is better than that of one; if the Church had a head,
Peter would be uneasy in the possession of
his power over her. The former of these two
reasons, taken strictly, would lead to nothing
less than the condemnation of monarchical government; and such certainly was not the
thought of Peter, who, not having wished for
a power shared by his brother and sister, was

---

* This abundantly proves that in recognising the emperor as
judge of the Synod, the members of this assembly do not speak
of themselves individually, but of the Synod as a constituted body.

† Bishops are now no longer drawn from the Synod. All the
members of this assembly are clothed with the episcopal character,
and placed at the head of a diocese, except two or three married
priests who cannot become bishops. But at the epoch of its foundation the Synod counted only three bishops, the president and
two vice-presidents. The four councillors and four assessors were
archimandrites and hegoumens, who naturally found themselves
on the high-road to the episcopate. Peter wished to have them
seen at work before conferring on them the episcopal character.

quite as decided to yield none of it to an assembly. We nevertheless believe in his sincerity. Power for him was not in question; it belonged to him, and only to him, such was his conviction. The question was only to secure instruments for exercising it. In this sense, it was in very good faith that he preferred collective government to that of a single person. Thus, instead of ministers, he had established *colleges* for foreign affairs, for war, for finance, &c. &c., and concentrated the whole administration in the senate.

When we cross the Place d'Isaac, and stop near the statue of Peter I., with the Neva flowing on our right, we see rise before us the two edifices in which assemble respectively the Synod and the Senate. This is the material realisation of Peter's thought. The two palaces are in the same line, have the same aspect, and form a symmetrical whole. Peter wished to govern the Church and the State by means of the Synod and the Senate; he caused himself to be equally represented in both assemblies, by a procurator assigned to each. Like those structures, which have been destroyed by the hand of time and rebuilt on a different plan, the organisation of Russia is no longer what it was a hundred and fifty years ago. The council of the empire has relegated the

Senate to the second plan, ministers have replaced the colleges; the Synod alone has remained standing in its isolation as a monument of the past, surviving the rest of the edifice of which it once formed a part. Under Peter's reign it was in perfect harmony with the other creations of the tsar reformer.

We think we have sufficiently unfolded Peter's idea, by saying that the government of several is better than that of one. The other argument, that it is more difficult for power to hold the Church in its hand when it has a single chief, needs no explication; 'tis the thought of the autocrat in all its clearness. He fully reckoned on remaining sole master; we shall see him later preëminently so.

In the other parts of the Ecclesiastical Regulation the lion-grip made itself less felt; it is perceptible that Prokopovich held the pen, but under his master's eye. This compilation has a double character; it is puerile and malignant.

First come ten pages in quarto, the points of which can be stated in few words. To make war on superstition: meaning by this certain prayers, lives of saints, images, relics, and miracles, which must be submitted to rigorous criticism. Then it is said that it would be very useful to make a little book, or catechism, con-

taining the exposition of the Symbol and De-
calogue, with selected homilies.* The bishops
shall read the canons, shall set themselves to
become acquainted with the degrees of consanguinity and affinity, from which arise hinder-
ances to marriage, and in doubtful cases they
will address themselves to the Synod. The
Synod will see whether it be proper to super-
sede them because of old age or sickness. They
shall build no useless churches, shall distrust
miraculous images, and combat superstitions.
They shall take care to found schools or seminaries, and to ordain as priests only those who
have been given to study. If the seminarists
are monks, they ought to be named archimandrites or hegoumens (abbots or priors), unless
they render themselves infamous by some great
crime (p. 33, n. 10). The bishops shall report
to the Synod the state of their revenues and of
those of the monasteries; they shall observe
economy and humility; shall pronounce no
excommunication without referring it to the
Synod; shall visit their dioceses every year or
every two years, receive any accusations made
against the clergy; assure themselves of the
state of the monasteries, much more by the
testimony of persons outside them than by that

* See, for the catechisms of the Russian Church, Tondini's
The Pope of Rome and the Popes, &c. pp. 81-94.

of the monks. Stress is laid on the necessity
of fighting against superstition, and on the dependence of the bishops on the Synod.

In the chapter on schools the Russian army
is given as a model, 'which was in so sad a
state before our very august and very puissant
monarch Peter I. introduced discipline into it.'
In order to prove the necessity of science, it is
said that during the first four centuries the
bishops had a horror of arrogance; but that
later they began to get proud, especially those
of Constantinople and Rome. From the year
500 to 1400 all Europe was plunged in darkness.

Then came the organisation of studies and
of seminaries; the rules for preachers; a distinction between laity and clergy obscure
enough; the Rascolniks, and how to treat them,
&c. The third part is devoted to the Synod
itself. This assembly shall watch that all bishops, priests, monks, laymen, discharge their
duties, and shall chastise those who do not.
Every one can address the Synod by writing.
No theological work can be printed without
its permission. When it is reported that a
dead body has been preserved from corruption,
or a miracle or vision been witnessed, the
Synod makes inquiry. It resolves cases of
conscience, examines bishops, satisfies itself of

their being neither superstitious nor impostors, informs itself as to the sources from which they can get money; it also judges them, and decides matrimonial causes and cases of divorce, and watches over the use of ecclesiastical property. The wills of important personages, in cases of doubt as to their validity, are examined by the Synod and by the College of Justice (Ministry of Justice).

Finally, the Regulation treats of mendicity. We do not find fault with their seeking to extirpate it by giving to the able-bodied poor the means of earning their living, and coming to the help of the rest; but we cannot without oppression of heart read these pages, every line of which breathes hatred of the poor. To give alms to an able-bodied pauper is to render oneself accessory to his sin. Mendicants are the greatest of scoundrels.* How can we help recalling the lesson in the Gospel? When John the Baptist, desiring to assure himself that Jesus was indeed the Messiah, sent some of his disciples to question Him, our Lord, in order to give the Forerunner proof that the Messiah was come, cites His own works, and says: *To the poor the Gospel is preached.* On reading the 'Spiritual Regulation,' and especially this

---

* ' Re quidem vera, non est hominum genus magis sceleratum profligatumque magis' (p. 98).

passage, which distils the venom of hatred against the poor, without meeting therein a word of compassion or charity, there can be no longer any doubt that it is not the Church that there speaks. Nor are the Russian people therein deceived, but in spite of the Synod continue to give alms.

In the supplement, among the rules given to the priests, we shall notice the 11th and 12th, which indicate in what cases the *confessor must reveal the secrets of the confessional.* If there be a plot against the emperor or the empire, or any machination against the honour or life of the emperor or his majesty's family, and the penitent be unwilling to abandon it; or still farther, if a false miracle be admitted as true, and the author of the imposture come to confess it, without, however, wishing to reveal it,—in these cases the confessor is bound to reveal the secret of the confessed and to denounce the guilty. The author of these strange rules says, in order to justify them, that false miracles expose the orthodox religion to the contempt of the heterodox. Alas! the pretended miracle of the Sacred Fire, which is performed every year at Jerusalem, and all the miracles that can be attributed to Metrophanes of Voronége, will never do so much harm to the Church as these 11th and 12th rules in the 'Spiritual Regulation.' Here again one cannot be deceived: it is not the voice of the Church, it is the invasion of the sanctuary by bureaucracy; but it is mournfully affecting to see bishops countersigning orders like these.*

Then come the rules for the monks. We shall refer to only one, the 36th, which forbids the monk to have a pen, *usus calami scriptorii, quantum ad extracta ex libris litterasque suasorias attinet, monachis denegatur.* The monk who shall have written without the abbot's permission shall undergo a severe corporal punishment, *sub gravi corporalis castigationis pœna.* It is equally forbidden to have ink and paper. Nothing is fraught with more danger to the monastic life than the rage for writing,

* History teaches us that the Russian clergy, both before and after the 'Spiritual Regulation,' did not much scruple to reveal the secrets of the confessional. During the trial of the Tsarevich Alexis, his confessor, Jaques Ignatieff, when put to the torture, June 19th, 1718, declared that the tsarevich had told him in confession that he had wished his father's death. On Oct. 12th, 1754, the priest Basil Sergueeff declared to the police that Barbe Joukoff had in confesion avowed to him that his mother had excited him to the murder of his mother-in-law. (*Russian Messenger*, Dec. 1860, p. 479.) The priest Gerbonovsky declared that the prisoner Striekha had in confession avowed to him such and such things. (Подъ Судъ (*Under Judgment*), published at London, August 1st, 1861.) Demetrius, Bishop of Rostoff (1651-1709), whom the Russian Church canonised, was obliged to rise up against the priests who reported what had been told them in confession. (Solovieff, *History of Russia*, vol. xv. p. 126.) These examples show that, in practice, little trouble was taken by the priests to set themselves above the restrictions indicated by the 'Spiritual Regulation.'

inanis et frivola scripturiendi prurigo. If, however, there are legitimate reasons for writing, and the abbot permit it, it shall be done in the refectory, and at the common inkstand. Any one daring to act otherwise will be severely punished, *contrarium ausuris severa pœna intentabitur.* This is a sad spectacle, but one full of instruction. This despot, this victor, this conqueror, has drowned in blood all resistance, not sparing even his own son; he has moulded his people like soft wax, recking naught of its traditions, customs, preferences; he has subjected the Church herself to his will, and Europe has proclaimed him great: yes, this man, who trembles in his solitary musings, see, he has caught a glimpse of one of those poor monks, who, shut up in their little cells, were there recording from day to day the history of their country. What would become of him, if in some corner of his immense empire one were to write the chronicles of Peter's reign? He who had faced all the artillery of Charles XII., what fears he? A book, a pamphlet, a journal, the liberty of the press? No; he is afraid of a pen in a monk's cell, and with reason; for the pen that defends the rights of truth and the freedom of the Church is stronger than he. But what also must be thought of the freedom and independence of the Russian

Church under the régime which Peter inaugurated ?

Let us cite two more rules relating to
monks. The apostle had written to Timothy,
'Let not a *widow* be chosen who is less than
sixty years old' (1 Tim. v. 9); the Synod made
it the rule of monasteries that *virgins* consecrated to God should not take their vows before
the age of sixty, and he quotes the authority of
St. Paul. The Synod, however, is appropriately
reminded that Peter's lawful wife is in a convent, and that the tsar might take it into his
head to send his second there—her to whom
he had just taken an oath of fidelity—before
she should reach the age of sixty. The Holy
Synod at once reserves to itself the power of
making *exceptions!*

Let us pass to the rule following the 43d,
which well deserves a literal translation. 'If
any young virgin still desire to embrace the
monastic life, in order to keep her virginity
perpetually, it is necessary to begin by carefully examining the circumstances. Does she
not wish to deceive? Is she not reduced to it
by reverses of fortune ? Is she not led away
by over-excitement?* Is it not the case of a

* We are not quite certain of having exactly understood the
sense of the text. The Latin is *Vel affectibus plus justo indulgeat.*
Of what excessive affections does it speak? We have supposed it
to mean an exalted mind.

person profoundly versed in the art of dissimu-
lation, who is feigning a wish to take the vow
of chastity ? If the examination is satisfactory,
she shall be sent into a convent distinguished
for the virtue of its nuns, and whose privacy
shall be carefully guarded ; she shall be placed
at the service of a nun of irreproachable conduct, and shall remain without assuming the
habit until the age of sixty, or fifty at the least.
If before this age the desire to be married
seize her, she shall be allowed to gratify it.'
' How perceptible that this was written by
those who had no faith in chastity, who mocked
at it and hated it ! Prokopovich doubtless
here still wielded the pen ; but among the signatures, beside his own, are found those of
three bishops, seven monks, and two priests.
We love to think that several among them, as
Stephen Yavorski and Theophylact Lopatinski,
signed through want of energy, without sharing the views of their colleagues.

Such is the ' Spiritual Regulation.'* It prescribes to confessors betrayal, forbids monks
the use of the pen, insults the chastity of those
virgins who wish to consecrate their virginity

---

* The above abstracts from the ' Spiritual Regulation' evince
how acceptable to all interested in Russian literature will be the
translation of that document from the original Russian, now being
prepared, with introduction and notes, by the Barnabite Fath. Tondini, under the auspices of the Paris Bibliographical Society. (*Tr.*)

to God; it has no bowels of compassion for the poor, and we look in vain for a single word breathing love to God or our neighbour; piety is as hateful to it as the independence of the Church; it desires not pastors but police agents—the blind instruments of power. If we Catholics, quite disinterested in all this, feel it difficult to restrain our indignation, what ought to be the sentiment of men obliged to avow themselves members of a Church in which this strange code has for 150 years had the force of law, and is unabrogated even now?

As to Synodal administration, it is a very complicated mechanism, which we can understand only by passing successively in review the Synod itself, its chief procurator, and the bureaux.

Peter's idea, we have seen, was that the Synod should consist of a bishop-president, two vice-presidents, equally bishops; four councillors and four assessors, taken from the clergy of the second order, regular and secular. To-day this is changed; no more president or vice-presidents, and all the members of the Synod are bishops, except two or three secular priests. One of these is the emperor's chaplain and confessor; the other is the chief chaplain of the army and navy. Admitted to the bosom of the Synod, the bishops retain the administration of their dioceses, however distant they may be from St. Petersburg.

In this assembly the members are distinguished into perpetual and temporary, the latter being called tó take part in the deliberations during a determinate period of time.

The metropolitans and the emperor's chaplain are always perpetual members, a distinction sometimes conferred on other bishops and on the chaplain-in-chief to the forces. One would from this be tempted to conclude that the perpetual members are irremovable, but 'tis not so ; the bishops can receive orders to return to their dioceses, and then, while retaining the title of members of the Synod, they cease to take part in its sittings. There is, however, a certain irremovability in fact for the Metropolitan of Petersburg and for the two chaplains ; but in an emergency these could always be got rid of; and as to the Metropolitan of Petersburg, it would not be impossible to transfer him to another see, or invite him *to take repose.*

The Synod, then, is composed just as the emperor pleases, and cannot become an element of opposition. In point of independence there is no comparison between an assembly of this kind and an irremovable patriarch. It is

also not a council. We are well aware that
M. Wassilieff, in his letter to Mgr. the Bishop
of Nantes, has had the courage to say that the
Synod 'is only the council of the Church of
Russia' (p. 33). This affirmation does not
bear examination; we confine ourselves to opposing to it the words of M. Katkoff, already
quoted above. ' The Holy Synod cannot take
the place of councils, because all the bishops
do not take part in its deliberations; whilst all
the bishops must absolutely sit in the provincial councils, such as were instituted by the
Apostles and by the œcumenical councils.'
(*Moscow Gazette*, 1866, No. 216.) Between
the council of the Russian Church and the
Synod there is the same difference as between
the English House of Peers and a commission
composed of half a dozen lords chosen by the
Queen. The minister who should bethink himself of maintaining that it is indifferent whether
we submit a law to the House of Peers or to
such a commission would be guilty of an enormous constitutional heresy. M. Wassilieff's
assertion is no less strange; and, for our part,
we believe the Synod itself but little disposed
to share the opinion of the Russian embassy's
ex-chaplain at Paris.

Not content with this dependence, Peter
took another guarantee, in the person of the

Synod's chief procurator. This personage 'has to sit in the assembly, and attentively watch that the Synod acquits itself of its functions, and that in all affairs subjected to its deliberations it proceed with truth, zeal, order, and without loss of time, *conformably to the regulations and ukases.* He must also attentively watch that the Synod acts with uprightness and without hypocrisy' (art. 1). 'He is to be considered as our own eye, and as the protector of state affairs; hence he should act with fidelity, for he in the first place will have to render an account' (art. 2). To find a man capable of discharging these functions, Peter recommends the selection from among the officers of a good man possessing boldness (ukase, May 11th, 1722). No decision is put in force without the chief procurator's consent. ' If he remark that the Synod is not acting with uprightness, but with hypocrisy, he is obliged instantly to point out to the Synod, clearly and with all necessary explanation, in what the Synod, or a part of it, are not acting properly, that they may correct it. And if they do not obey, he must thereupon protest, stop the deliberation on the matter, and report it to us at once, if it be of great importance; otherwise, when we come to the Synod, or in the course of the month or of the week ' (Instr. art. 2).

Many matters subject to the deliberation of
the Synod must besides be referred to the emperor.   In this case the chief procurator draws
up the report, presents it, accompanying it
with the needful explanation, and transmits
the supreme decision to the Synod.

The chief procurator is, then, a real intermediary minister between the emperor and the
Synod.   He has under his orders: 1st, his
own chancery; 2d, that of the Synod; 3d, the
central direction of the ecclesiastical schools;
4th, the directory charged with administration
and revenue.   The *personnel* of all these offices is placed under his control; nominations,
promotions, dismissions, all depend on him.
The central direction of the ecclesiastical schools
is a veritable ministry of public instruction for
the clergy.   The directory of administration
and revenue is chiefly occupied with finance,
with what may be called the clergy-chest.   The
authority exercised by the chief procurator over
all these administrations naturally gives him
great influence on the progress of affairs submitted to the Synod, as also over diocesan
authorities.   We have seen that he was in direct correspondence with the consistory secre-
taries, who, on a smaller theatre, play at these
ecclesiastical assemblies the same part that the
chief procurator does at the Synod.   Farther,

all these administrations are obliged to send
to the Synod or to the chief procurator a very
large number of reports, accounts, and papers
of all sorts. A delay in sending these papers,
an irregularity in digesting them, expose the
diocesan authorities to receive from the chief
procurator demands for explanation or rectifi-
cation, reproaches, sometimes even reprimands.
It is easy to understand how by these thousand
bonds the diocesan authorities find themselves
in dependence on him.

But 'tis necessary that we enter into some
detail, in order to clearly show how bureaucracy has invaded the Church and entwined
her in its meshes.

Papers of every kind addressed to the Synod go to the chancery. They are read, sum-
marised, reported on in connection with the
articles of law applying to them. On the Synod's assembling, extracts from the report are
read, and pertinent legal texts. Thereupon
begins the discussion, which terminates in the
adoption of a resolution in such or such a sense :
this resolution is put in writing, and signed by
all the members. They are besides obliged to
sign the minutes of the sittings, and a great
number of other papers. If we calculate the
number of matters submitted every year to the
decision of the Synod, and the number of hours

it is in session, we reach the conclusion that it can on an average give but five minutes to each matter. Now there are matters so very complicated as to demand the perusal of many hundreds of pages, and give rise to long discussions. Here, then, is a physical impossibility. In the majority of cases discussion is suppressed, the sentence being drawn up beforehand by the chancery, and the members required only to sign it. This process, however, is still too long; the chancery is empowered to set aside all affairs of little moment. Of these not even the report is read, the papers already drawn up being merely presented to the members of the Synod for signature. Their signatures are even frequently gathered one after another at their homes. To read these papers, one would suppose that all were the work of the Synod, and transacted during its sessions. From this state of things it is evident that the greater part of the business is decided on in the government offices by the subordinate officials. It even sometimes happens that the chancery takes upon itself to entirely change a decision which has been arrived at in session. In this case the great thing is to obtain a first signature at some member's house, which usually draws after it all the rest. It is very evident to all that the decision is quite different from the one taken in the sitting; but they can suppose that the chief procurator refused to sanction the decision taken, and that, in consequence, the resolution was changed. For peace' sake they sign; the chief procurator, having on an average one hundred signatures per day to write, has often nothing to do with it; and this abuse of authority emanates purely and simply from the chancery.

Some years ago a privy councillor, a director of the chancery of the Synod, was condemned to deportation to Siberia for malversations. All the employés of the chancery are not, then, incorruptible, and an idea can thus be formed of the abuses resulting from this omnipotence of the bureaux.

There is a story that a member of the Synod seeing one of his colleagues reading a paper, said to him, 'Stop, we are not here to read, but to sign; sign now, it gives less trouble, and is sooner done.' On one occasion, when a resolution taken during a sitting had been changed for one totally different, one of the most important personages of the chancery repaired to a member of the Synod and obtained his signature. Another made more difficulty about it. 'Why do you trouble yourself? said the official to him. He who is most directly

interested in the matter has made no objection.
Look at his signature.' The old man signed;
but one of his confidants, entering some mo-
ments after, found him bathed in tears. 'My
God! my God!' cried he, 'to what a depth of
humiliation are we fallen!'*

Besides the chancery, the chief procurator
has still under his orders the central direction
of the ecclesiastical schools; and if a little more
authority over their seminaries has been given
to the bishops, the central direction, which always maintains a high hand, is itself placed in
the most entire dependence on the chief procurator. The Synod exercises a certain, but very
restricted, control; it can but feebly oppose the
procurator, and besides presents but little co-
hesion.

Fancy all the Catholic seminaries of a country placed under the supervision and control of
a council composed of five or six bishops named
by the minister of worship, able to take no
step without the *visa* of this minister, with lay
bureaux having in their hands all the correspondence and manipulating all the business.
Catholic bishops would never admit the mere
possibility of such an organisation; yet how
many more guarantees would they have in the

* О правосл. бѣломъ и черномъ духов. tom. ii. pp. 1-20: On the
Synod, the chief procurator, and the chancery.

present state of civilisation which are altogether
wanting to the Russian bishops !

The department of revenue exercises its
action over all financial and material matters.
Herein, to pass by all else, all diocesan authorities find themselves under the chief procurator's control, who experiences no difficulty in
making them feel his authority.

It is curious, after this, to hear the archpriest Wassilieff say to Mgr. the Bishop of
Nantes : ' You see, Mgr., that far from being
the president of the holy Synod, the chief procurator is not even a member of it ; he is simply but a civil functionary at the council. Far
from being the Church's master and oppressor,
he is its benefactor and servant.'*

After these decisive proofs of the dependence of the Russian clergy in presence of the
procurator of the Synod, it must be granted that
all precautions have been taken against anything being either said or done in the Russian
Church but with the consent and approval of
the State, as represented by the chief procurator.
Have the same precautions been taken against
the State's encroachments on the Church ? This
does not appear to have been dreamt of. *The*

* *Discussion entre Mgr. l'Evêque de Nantes et M. l'Archiprêtre
Wassilieff au sujet de l'Autorité dans l'Eglise de Russie.* Paris,
1861, pp. 71, 72.

Free Church in the Free State is certainly not the formula expressing the position of the Russian Church ; no, we must seek for some other.

What we have hitherto said sufficiently explains why we should ask in vain whether of the Russian government or of the Patriarch of Constantinople, or of the Synod itself, or finally of the organs of public opinion, their sincere judgment of the institution of the Synod. Yet we should attach the highest value to knowing exactly what they think of it. Really this is not, perhaps, as impossible as one would think it. Peter I. has had imitators, and among the number those who for some reason or other do not inspire the same reserve, and in whom one does not much hesitate to blame that which one admires in him. Such, among others, is Prince Couza, till lately Hospodar of Wallachia and Moldavia, who treated the Church cavalierly enough, without however taking so many liberties with her as Peter I. did with the Russian Church. Now, we are so fortunate as to possess on Couza's unlucky reforms the opinions of the Patriarch of Constantinople, of the Russian Synod, of the Russian government, of the Russian journals, and, lastly, that of the actual chief procurator of the Synod. It will be sufficient to translate from the Russian a few documents taken from the journals. Let us begin with the *Northern Post*,* the official journal of the Minister of the Interior, and see how it sums up and criticises Prince Couza's acts relative to the Roumanian Church:

'In order to make understood the documents we publish below, it is indispensable to glance at the acts of the late Prince Couza relative to the orthodox Church in the Principalities.

We know that Prince Couza sought support in the ranks of the enemies of orthodoxy, and for this he sought to subordinate to his authority the Roumanian orthodox clergy and the administration of the Church. To attain this end, Prince Couza thought to introduce new ecclesiastical institutions of such a nature as to completely weaken the Church while subjecting it to his power.

By his orders there were drawn up at the Ministry of Public Worship, without the coöperation of the clergy, three projects of new ecclesiastical regulations, which in July 1864 received the sanction of the Parliament, and at the end of the year were signed by the Hospodar. Of this new code the principal features are these:

The Roumanian orthodox Church (which hitherto depended on the hierarchical supremacy of the Patriarch of Constantinople) is proclaimed independent of all foreign ecclesiastical authority whatsoever. The government of the Roumanian Church is subject to a Synod receiving the denomination, hitherto unheard of among the orthodox, of *General Synod*. Of this Synod are named as members, firstly, all the Roumanian bishops; then three delegates from each diocese, chosen for three years among the priests or laymen, but by such a mode of election that the re-

* Сѣверная Почта.

sult of the scrutiny depends on the will of the government. The presidency of the Synod is conferred on the Metropolitan of Wallachia, but not in virtue of the dignity with which he is clothed, nor in his own name; but *in the name of the Hospodar*, a thing unheard of in the orthodox as well as in the Latin Church.

The Synod must assemble in July once every two years; it is convoked by the Minister of Public Worship, who proposes the questions for debate, is present at its sittings, takes part in its deliberations, presents its resolutions to the Hospodar, and puts them into execution. If the Synod presumes to touch any matter not brought before it, the minister terminates the sitting. In any case of urgency for the immediate convoking of an extraordinary sitting, the bishops must address their request for it to the minister, with whom it lies to grant or to refuse it. The Synod has no right to extend its supervision to the instruction in the seminaries (so that Latin tendencies could be there propagated without hindrance). The Synod has no right to meddle in judgment as to the measures relating to toleration and liberty of conscience which the civil power shall deem it useful to adopt (in order to open the gates to Roman propagandism).

To complete these measures, by order of the Hospodar, the Chamber, in January 1865, sanctioned another project relating to the nomination of bishops. There had long existed a rule inscribed in the law of Moldavia and Wallachia, in virtue of which the bishops are elected in assemblies composed of ecclesiastical and lay deputies, and afterwards confirmed by the Hospodar; as to the election of the metropolitans, it is subject to the confirmation of the Patriarch of Constantinople. In contempt of this ancient rule, it has been established that the bishops and metropolitans should be chosen in a preliminary assembly of the council of ministers, and that they should be desig-

nated by the Hospodar on the presentation of the minister of worship. In this fashion the Hospodar completely
possessed himself of the government of the Church, he
arrogated to himself the right of naming her bishops and
controlling all their dispositions.

To crown all these innovations, it has been laid down
by a special article, that "all previous laws not agreeing
with the present dispositions are abrogated." By these
last words the force and authority of all the canons of the
œcumenical councils, forming the basis of the organisation,
administration, and life of the orthodox Church, are definitively broken.

The news of the accomplishment of these reforms arrived in Constantinople by the *Courrier de Dacie,* which
published the text of the new laws; it there produced in-
tense excitement, and indeed profound grief, in all orthodox society. His Holiness the Patriarch Sophronius convoked an extraordinary council, in which all patriarchs
happening to be in the city took part, both those in office
and those deposed, all metropolitans, all bishops, and a
few archimandrites. This assembly adopted a conciliary
canonical resolution on the essential signification of the
new legislative measures, and on the usurpation of the
Roumanian government in matters ecclesiastical. It was
resolved to transmit it to Bucharest, by sending there the
archimandrite Eustachius Cleobulus with letters from the
Patriarch for the Hospodar, the Metropolitans of Wallachia and Moldavia, as also for all the bishops under
them, demanding the repeal of the newly promulgated
ecclesiastical laws.

Every one knows from the journals the result of the
archimandrite Cleobulus's journey: under the pretext of
no leisure amid his numerous engagements, the ex-Prince
Couza refused for a fortnight to receive the Patriarch's
envoy, and at last sent him word to hand the papers he

had brought to the minister of worship, notwithstanding the persistency of Father Cleobulus, who had declared that he had a mission from the Patriarch to deliver by word of mouth certain communications to the Hospodar.

After this, in order to put an end to his sojourn in the Principalities, he was accused of fomenting plots and an insurrection against the government ; and under this pretext, police-agents were sent to him, who, having searched his papers through without finding anything, hurried him under escort beyond the frontiers to the city of Giurgevo ; here, after having undergone another examination, and whilst waiting for the steamboat, he was shut up in a room and sentinels placed at his door. The Patriarch's envoy, thus humiliated and insulted, did not wait for the steamer ; but hurrying into a fisherman's boat, crossed the Danube, and betook himself to Rustchuk.

In this ignominious fashion was the archimandrite Cleobulus driven from Bucharest, May 11th ; and on the same day, as a reply to the Patriarch's letter, Prince Couza, of his own authority, designated the six first bishops for the vacant sees in Roumania, and among the number the Metropolitan of Moldavia.

The return of the archimandrite Cleobulus produced at Constantinople a general outburst of indignation among the clergy and orthodox population ; for in the annals of the orthodox Church was there no example of the official envoy of the first and most ancient of her pastors having received a reception so outrageous, contemptuous, and insolent, on the part of a ruler of an orthodox, and above all of a *little* country,—one not independent, but whose prince was vassal to another ; and when, farther, the prince of the Church in the country he governs is hierarchically subordinate directly to this pastor.*

* We have reproduced as textually as we could this very tangled phrase, the sense of which is, however, very clear. The *Northern*

The Patriarch immediately convoked a new extraordinary council, and communicated to it the result of the mission with which the archimandrite Cleobulus had been charged. The council decided that in these circumstances, painful and important for the whole orthodox Church, it was necessary to ask counsel of the other national orthodox Churches. For two months the Church of Constantinople waited for the Hospodar's answer to the Patriarch's letter; but when this expectation proved vain, there was no longer room for delay or for tenderness towards the Roumanian government. His Holiness sent to our [of Russia] plenipotentiary at Constantinople, to procure the sending to the holy Synod an official letter, asking of it wise counsel, fraternal support, and salutary measures, within the limits of the rights determined by the canons, in order to put an end to the perilous situation of the Moldo-Wallachian Church.

The Hospodar, however, and his devoted accomplices did not sleep, and in order to justify before European public opinion the usurpation they had permitted in ecclesiastical affairs, and their unheard-of proceedings in respect to the Patriarch's enyoy, had recourse to the press. News from Bucharest appeared in the foreign journals, according to which, the true cause of the disagreements between the Church and the Roumanian government was simply the material constraint in which the Patriarch found himself in consequence of the confiscation in the Principalities of the monastic properties belonging to the Greek Church; a report being at the same time spread that the archimandrite Cleobulus had been sent to Bucharest with the object of

---

Post intended to say, 'Were it the Emperor of Russia, nothing could be said; but the Hospodar of Wallachia!' And this observation well attests the rare prudence of the *Poste du Nord;* for there is no other difference.

raising there an insurrection against the government. In these circumstances people did not forget to calumniate Russia; but the journal *Byzantis*, the organ of the Patriarch of Constantinople, reëstablished the facts as they were, and, starting with the unjust attacks directed against Russia, recalled to notice the ingratitude with which her benefits to Moldo-Wallachia had been requited by the men at the head of the Roumanian government. The ex-Hospodar, Prince Couza, again had recourse to a peculiar means of bringing public opinion to his side in the matter. He drew up an answer to the Patriarch's letter; but without sending it to him, had it printed in the foreign journals.

This answer, written in defence of the anti-canonical innovations introduced into the Roumanian Church, consisted in an arbitrary interpretation of the ecclesiastical canons, and in inexact references to historical facts which were either distorted or meant absolutely nothing. By this subterfuge the public, but little familiar with these canons and facts, and having no idea of the contents of the Patriarch's letter, after having acquainted themselves with the Hospodar's reply, which was not remarkable for its veracity, were obliged to consider Prince Couza's acts perfectly regular.

The Roumanian clergy could not remain a silent and indifferent witness of this abuse of power on the part of the government.* Deprived of force and influence, it dared not loudly protest against the Hospodar's acts; but on May 23d the bishops presented to Prince Couza a memorial signed by them, in which, in the most humble terms, but nevertheless with much detail and firmness, they pronounced a complete censure on the ecclesiastical laws newly published, and prayed the Prince not to put them in execution, but to previously submit them to the examination of the bishops in order to their modification.

* *Northern Post*, you forget yourself!

No regard was paid to this petition. Several of the bishops then addressed themselves by private letters directly to the Patriarch of Constantinople, imploring his defence in favour of the unfortunate Church of Roumania, and speaking of the excommunication of Prince Couza, whom they dubbed Julian the Apostate. Two bishops, quitting the Principalities, undertook a pilgrimage to Jerusalem and Mount Athos, to avoid taking part in innovations to which their duty and conscience were alike repugnant.*

When Prince Couza and his accomplices learnt that the Patriarch had addressed himself officially to the *most holy* Synod of the Russian Church, and to the *holy* Synod of Athens,† for their advice, they were terrified at sight of the peril which threatened them. By virtue of the canons, the authors of violence against the Church, and those who infringe her laws, are excommunicated; and in the present case a resolution on this subject, taken by all the Eastern patriarchs, with the full powers of the Russian and Athenian Synods, would have been a determination taken in common by all the parts of the orthodox Church, and would have been equivalent to the sentence of an œcumenical council. To prevent these consequences, the Hospodar ordered his chargé-d'affaires at Constantinople immediately to send the Patriarch Sophronius the reply to the latter's letter long since published in the journals. The chargé-d'affaires multiplied to the Patriarch excuses and regrets respecting what had happened, and sought to justify Prince Couza, by saying that he had acted against his own feelings and convictions under the pressure of circumstances. In concluding, he expressed in the warmest terms the liveliest desire on the part of the Hospodar to

---

* If the Russian bishops of Peter the First's time had acted in this fashion, they would perhaps have deserved the eulogies of the *Northern Post;* but they would have expired on the wheel.

† The little cannot be *most* holy.

arrange this affair by putting himself in accord with his
Holiness, and, to this end, to enter into negotiations with
him. This proposition of Prince Couza had, however, no
result. The Patriarch then judged it necessary once more
to convoke the council, which decided that a new letter
ought to be addressed to the Hospodar, refuting the in-
correct conclusions contained in his reply, and inviting
him into the path of regular conduct. In the following
November the Patriarch sent a copy of these documents
to our most holy Synod, with a letter, in which he requested its concurrence for the defence of the spiritual interests of the Roumanian people.

At this same epoch the Roumanian government announced the convocation of the General Synod at Bucharest for the month of December, and occupied itself with
preparing the programme of its labours. As all the acts
of Prince Couza and his party had for their object to de-
tach the Roumanian Church from the œcumenical, they
were incessantly devising new measures for successively
separating the people from orthodoxy, and subjecting them
to the Pope by means of the union.* An attempt of this
kind is seen in the series of questions sent by the minis-

* We have no concern here with the plan pursued by Prince
Couza, but we cannot refrain from saying that the *Northern Post*
is misled in imagining that this Hospodar laboured in the interest
of the Catholic Church. Prince Couza wished to substitute in the
Roumanian Church the Latin rite for the Greek—this we believe—
taking this course on the ground that the Roumanians were a Latin
race; but he certainly did not dream of subjecting the Roumanian
Church to the authority of the Pope. He wished for a national
Church, as independent of Rome as of Constantinople. If the *Poste
du Nord* aims at knowing what this Church was to be, it can ask
Prince Vladimir Tcherkasky, who now has leisure to communicate
to it the plans he formed for the Polish Church. The Roumanian
Church of Prince Couza and the Polish Church of Prince Tcherkasky were to be constructed on the same plan : a Latin rite ; absolute independence of Rome ; absolute dependence on the civil power.

ter of worship to one of the bishops designated by the Hospodar, and which were to be submitted to the Synod for deliberation. Among these questions figured the introduction of the Gregorian Calendar into general use, and into that of the Church, and the adoption of organs in churches. A year before, there had been inserted in the *Voice of Roumania,* a journal subsidised by the government, certain articles which, by the aid of false statements and perverted historical facts, led one to give to Latinism the character of the national religion of Roumania.

At Jassy a Latin seminary was organised, with the aid of government, in which was given instruction incomparably superior to that of the orthodox seminaries; for in the latter, not even instruction in classical and modern languages was permitted, in order that the orthodox clergy might stand on a lower level than the Latin. The prelate Salanderi was allowed to enter Moldavia as a visitor sent by the Pope, and a report even got into circulation that the Hospodar was continually carrying on negotiations with the Court of Rome, but that these were wrapt in impenetrable mystery.

At the time of the convocation of the Synod, the intentions and views of the government were clearly manifested with respect to the results expected from this measure. In article 4 of the new law, it was said that all the bishops are members of the General Synod; but Prince Couza caused letters of convocation to be addressed only to a certain number of bishops chosen according to considerations of his own. Two Moldavian bishops, Mgr. Joseph of Sebaste, and Mgr. Filaret of Stauropol, known for their devotion to orthodoxy, having received no invitation to sit in the Synod, resolved, notwithstanding, to repair to Bucharest; but they were stopped on the road by agents of the government, and sent back under escort from Fokchany to Jassy. They forwarded their protests to the consuls of the protecting powers, as well as in the name of the General Synod. In these documents they strongly complained of the usurpation of the Hospodar, and of the innovations he had introduced into the Church. Mgr. Neophyte, Bishop of Edessa, and brother of the Bishop of Stauropol, also sent a protest. This proceeding of the three bishops, and the sympathy they met with among the members of the Synod, excited in that assembly a strong opposition to all the Latin innovations, in spite of the predominating influence of governmental authority. In consequence of this circumstance, and fearing new conflicts on spiritual matters, the Hospodar resolved on closing the session for an indefinite time. The orthodox people of Roumania will doubtless know well how to discern the motives which have brought about these innovations, and will not allow themselves to be seduced by the manifest imposture of the enemies of their Church and nationality.

In presence of acts so grievous for the orthodox Church, emanating from the government of the late Prince Couza, the most holy Synod could not but answer with entire sympathy the fraternal letter addressed to it by the œcumenical Patriarch.' (*Mosc. Gaz.* 1866, No. 43, Feb. 26, o.s.)

We have translated the entire article of the *Northern Post*, as given in the *Moscow Gazette*, leaving the official sheet of St. Petersburg to exhibit Prince Couza's acts from its own point of view. These we by no means pretend to defend; but we ask ourselves, how is it possible to have two weights and two measures, and so blame in Prince Couza what is praised in Peter I. ? If we go to the root of the matter, Couza has done no more than follow the example set him on the banks of the Neva. He has perhaps a little less skilfully disguised his usurpation, but it does not outdo what has been done at Petersburg; in both cases we see a national Church completely independent of all foreign control, and completely subject to the civil power. It would even be easy to demonstrate that, in several respects, the Roumanian Church had preserved guarantees utterly wanting in the case of the Russian Church. Suffice it to mention the irremovability of the bishops. The *General Synod* of Bucharest is no greater innovation than that (governing) Synod of St. Petersburg; both are far from canonical, but the composition of that at Bucharest assured to it a considerable degree of independence, as the event has proved. The only real difference between these two ecclesiastical *coups d'état* is that so accurately indicated by the *Northern Post* itself: in the one case we see a petty vassal-prince of the sultan's, in the other a powerful autocrat. The *Northern Post* has forgotten to tell us in what this difference, very real in a military and political point of view, has any value in a canonical.

But it is time to allow the Patriarch of Constantinople to speak.

'To the most holy governing Synod of the Orthodox

Church of the empire protected of God in all the Russias, our fraternal greeting in Jesus Christ.

Without doubt, reports have reached your Reverences of the projects of law of the Roumanian government, which, contrary to all expectation, have lately appeared, and which, by introducing changes into the ecclesiastical administration of the orthodox Principalities of the Danube, with the object of shaking the foundations of the piety of the orthodox Roumanian people, transmitted by their fathers, by means of the enslavement of the holy clergy of this country, by means of usurpation by the lay power of ecclesiastical rights, and by all kinds of attempts to introduce anti-canonical innovations, as is known to all those who have attentively followed the under-mentioned projects of law, which also have already been published in the journals. Having early become acquainted with such a state of affairs in these countries, the great and holy Church of Christ, the spiritual guardian of the commandments of the Apostles and holy Fathers, took care more than a year ago to put on his guard the spiritual pastor of this country, Mgr. Niphon, Metropolitan of the Hungaro-Wallachian Church, by transmitting to him in our synodical letter the necessary counsels and instructions, which unfortunately were not accepted by his Grace with the dispositions and zeal they deserved, because he allowed himself to be led by the suggestions of political authority, as we have learnt by the reply he has at last sent us, and by other indications. Consequently, being acquainted with the aforesaid projects of law, the great Church of Christ, accomplishing the duty, imposed on her by the canons, of watching over the Church of this country, being unable to remain an indifferent spectator of things having for their object the spiritual ruin of her pious children, resolved to convoke a great and holy council, composed of most holy patriarchs, venerated metropolitans, and most reverend doctors ; and this council, after a severe and attentive ex- amination, has formulated a decree, in which, by means of testimonies borrowed from Scripture and the canons, it unmasks the anti-canonical character of the laws projected by the Roumanian government, and exposes with a spi- ritual prudence the necessity of abrogating and annulling them. This synodical decree, accompanied by ecclesiasti- cal letters, has been sent into Moldo-Wallachia, to the re- presentatives of the two powers, through an ecclesiastical personage, to whom has been confided the mission not only of officially delivering these documents, but farther of explaining them in case of need, in conformity with the spirit of the Church. Your venerable charity will be able to take an exact and detailed notice of these important dispositions of the great Church of Christ, by the copies which we transmit you under this cover. You will there find the copy of the synodical letter to the Metropolitan of the Hungaro-Wallachian Church, which was written on the occasion of the reports being circulated of the abolition of the Old Calendar, adopted by the Oriental Church ; on the recitation of the symbol with the addition condemned by the œcumenical councils, as well as by the above-named resolution, and by the letters added thereto, as also the copy of the last reply of the said metropolitan, dispatched by himself after the return of the ecclesiastical personage sent by the Church. But what trouble will not your mind feel when you learn the reception accorded by his Highness Prince Alexander Couza to the expressed solici- tude of the great Church of Christ,* inspired by her ma- ternal grief ! His Highness did not deign to receive and hear the envoy of the great Church of Christ : our archi- mandrite, a very worthy man, known for his piety and learning, was with great ignominy sent back beyond the frontiers of the Principalities under guard of the police.

* This is the title taken by the Church of Constantinople.

To crown so many outrages, calumnies without number have been spread abroad about his sojourn and his embassy, which had a character purely ecclesiastical; and our patriarchal and synodical letters addressed to his Highness have been contemned, and not been honoured even with an answer. Nor was this enough : immediately after the envoy's expulsion, the *pious* (!) prince confirmed the above-mentioned projects of law, and he, a temporal prince, placed at the head of Churches bishops chosen by the ministry.

This, beloved brethren in Christ, is the reason why we have deemed it necessary to inform you of these things, that you may receive an exact account of the circumstances of the matter, in order to judge in common of the determination of the great Church of Christ, which has condemned as contrary to the canons, and transgressing the eternal limits set by our fathers, the said projects of law of the Roumanian government trenching on spiritual and ecclesiastical matters entirely foreign to its jurisdiction. We are convinced that in the present matter, which demands union and unanimity of all the orthodox Churches in Jesus Christ, your venerated charity, sharing not only the profound grief and the painful impression felt by us, and by all orthodox Christian hearts, at this conduct of the Roumanian government, but also the solicitude inspiring us for the salvation of the orthodox Roumanian people exposed to so great a danger, will doubtless be willing to consider and examine everything that can conduce to this end, and will not fail to take, with suitable care, and within the limits fixed by the canons, all other salutary measures to render vain those efforts against which the Church of Christ has in the spirit of gentleness striven until now. Thus we await from you not only the expression of your serious attention, and the judgment of your pious wisdom, but farther your fraternal coöperation, and the spiritual help with which religious zeal will inspire you, to put an end to so dangerous a situation, which is dragging into perdition a Christian people for whose blood we must hereafter give account. We shall await with impatience your esteemed reply, and news of your brotherly health, which is precious to us.

The Lord grant you long years, health, and salvation.

Your Reverences' very dear and loving brother in Jesus Christ, Sophronius of Constantinople.'

We have endeavoured to give the most literal translation possible of this curious document. We will not dwell on the rather hollow phraseology, and the little agreement between words and deeds; but we will openly congratulate ourselves on seeing the Church of Constantinople proclaim with so much earnestness the necessity of maintaining ecclesiastical independence in the presence of the secular power, and the union of the different national Churches, to form therefrom one single universal Church.

Let us now see the reply of the Synod. We must be just to this assembly. It felt itself in a false position, and, spite of itself, to this feeling its embarrassed language testifies.

'To the most holy Sophronius, Archbishop of Constantinople,—the new Rome,—œcumenical Patriarch.

Fraternal greeting in our Lord Jesus Christ.

By the letter of your Holiness, dated July 1st, 1865, we have learnt with profound grief the events which have afflicted all the united Churches in orthodoxy, and which have shaken the good order and prosperity of the Moldo-Wallachian Church.

If our sympathising thought has stopped on the, road that leads to word and action (that is, if we have as yet neither said nor done anything), it has been partly for want of knowing with clearness and precision certain circumstances of these events, and partly because we were hoping that the orthodox spirit of the ministers of the Moldo-Wallachian Church would be aroused, would with firmness place itself on guard of the ancient ecclesiastical order handed down by the fathers ; that they would raise a persuasive voice towards the orthodox authorities and towards the people ; that they would take to heart the voice of the Mother Church, and by these common efforts be preserved from innovations incompatible with the sacred canons.

It is to us a new affliction to see our hopes little justified by the course of events. The members of the Moldo-Wallachian hierarchy are but few who, not without suffering, have uttered words of truth in order to unmask error : may their sacrifice be pleasing to the divine Head of the Church, the Christ, our God! The Moldo-Wallachian Prince has not, most holy sir, deigned to reply to your letter, and to the memorial of the council surrounding you, with pacific dispositions, but has decided, according to his own expression, "to fight them with the invincible arms of the laws and canons."

In these circumstances, in virtue of our duty to guard in common and mutually the peace and unanimity of the Churches, we find ourselves obliged to testify that the war undertaken has not been marked by victory, and that the right arrogated by the temporal prince, to innovate in the legislation and administration of the Moldo-Wallachian Church, appears destitute of legal basis. The detailed exposition of this thought is given in the annexed dissertation.

We recognise that the establishment of a new Synod, having legislative and administrative authority, is beyond the competence of the civil power, and demands the examination and confirmation of a council more exalted in the Church, and particularly that of the Patriarch to whose jurisdiction the Church instituting a new Synod belongs. Examples of this can be seen at hand in the Synod of all the Russias, and in that of Athens. We recognise as contrary to the canons and to the Gospel (Luke x. 16, Matt. xviii. 20), the proposition that "The Metropolitan of Roumania presides at the Synod in the name of the Hospodar." We recognise as contrary to the canons, the designation of bishops by sole lay authority without ecclesiastical election. Those who have been nominated in this fashion should confront the 30th canon of the holy Apostles, and examine with fear if it be a veritable consecration which they will receive and extend over their flock.

We confine ourselves to noting the most important deviations from the sacred canons. If God's grace bring about a return from these to the Church's true path, it will also reveal the means of remedying the rest. Without doubt, most holy sir, your paternal love for the Moldo-Wallachian Church and her children is not exhausted. Could not means be found by a persuasive and love-inspired language to sustain those who are now strong in justice, to strengthen those who are shaken, bring back those who have wandered, replace the matter on the ground of pacific conference, and guarantee the inviolability of what is essential by some condescension as to what can be tolerated? We are convinced that in order to arrive at this result, our most pious emperor will order, or has already ordered, his minister to transmit to the Moldo-Wallachian government good and pacific counsels.

We pray our Lord Jesus Christ, by His all-influencing grace, to direct your acts, and those of the council assem-

bled around you, to the pacification of the Moldo-Wallachian Church, and to the preservation of this member of
Christ's mystical body in a healthful union with the great
body of the orthodox œcumenical Church. We sincerely
wish your Holiness every good with salvation, and remain
united to you in the bonds of brotherly love in Jesus
Christ.'

It will be remarked, even from the Synod's
avowal, that its answer is conformed to the
diplomatic note emanating from the minister
of foreign affairs. It is useless to ask if the
Synod dictated the note, or the Minister the
reply. Besides, the Synod was obliged to lean
to the side of concession; it could not, without
condemning itself, pronounce anathema against
its own founder.

As a sequel to these three important documents, let us farther reproduce the article of
the *Moscow Gazette:*

' We this day publish some documents of a very extraordinary character. They are the letter of the most holy
Patriarch of Constantinople to the most holy Synod of
Russia, and the reply of the latter. We have called these
documents extraordinary; and truly, who is there that remembers the publication of any relations whatsoever of
general interest between the Russian hierarchy and the
other branches of the œcumenical Church? In different
countries there exist Churches, calling themselves Oriental
Catholic; but between them there is no bond or settled
relations. They have no organisation vindicating to them
their œcumenical character. We see Churches which, alas!

already begin profoundly to differ from one another in their modes of regarding many very essential objects; but an œcumenical Church such as each of these ought to be exists only in an idea ever receding into obscurity, and losing all connection with reality. This is the great question which long ago made itself felt within our Church, and which will soon appear in all its strength. We must be prepared for it. 'Tis time that the zealots of our Church cease to see in her only a national institution; to recall to themselves her œcumenical character constituting her essence, which is above and more precious than all the rest. The Church of Christ and orthodoxy must not be made to consist in the peculiarities of an organisation constituted in this or that country, under the influence of different circumstances often the most unfavourable; or also in things accidental, which often darken and disfigure the essence of religion, and in every case have nothing in common with her; or in the architectural character of churches, in the form of images, in the number of buttons on sacerdotal vestments; or again, in the mode of joining the fingers of the hand to make the sign of the cross; or again, in the educational establishments for the daughters of the clergy (as if children, or, in general, persons not in fact attached to the service of the altar, could form a part of the clergy); finally, in a clergy understood in the sense of a caste and race apart.

But we have no intention to touch to-day on great ecclesiastical questions, nor even to examine the proceeding between the Patriarch of Constantinople and the fallen Hospodar of the Danubian Principalities. We wish to call attention to but a single circumstance which throws a very bright light on our own affairs. The correspondence of the Patriarch of Constantinople with our Synod is preceded by an official statement of the events which gave rise to it. We see developed the long series of violent and ma-

levolent measures of the ex-Hospodar of Moldavia and
Wallachia, which sought to humble and overthrow the
orthodox Church. Not content with subjecting the Church
and hierarchy to all imaginable oppressions, Prince Couza
aimed at destroying the dominant Church in its root, *i.e.*
in the formation of its clergy. Taking care to organise in
the best possible manner the Roman Catholic seminaries,
he applied himself at the same time to give to the orthodox
seminaries the worst organisation possible; he forbade
them instruction in the ancient languages, "with the object of placing the orthodox clergy on a comparatively
lower educational level than that of the Latin clergy." The
official statement forming the introduction to the documents calls attention to this circumstance, as crowning the
series of malevolent measures taken by the ex-Hospodar.
Without question, Prince Couza knew what he was about.
He did not hide his designs. He acted as an enemy, and
his acts corresponded—none better—to his intentions.
His adversaries had every reason to point out in their
indictment this systematic deterioration of the houses of
education, which he had deprived of the classic languages
as the most pedagogic and palpable of means. But in at-
tacking Prince Couza in this fashion, what shall we say of
ourselves? He acted as an enemy, he wished to destroy
all instruction of the orthodox clergy; and to this end, as
the official statement justly observes, he took away from
the orthodox seminaries the foundation of a classical education.

Why then, we ask, is absolutely the same thing done
in Russia? If the acts of the minister of worship and
public instruction in Roumania become a ground for accusation; if we see these malevolent and hostile acts; what
must be said of the reforms our seminaries underwent in
1840, and our gymnasia in 1848? What of the efforts
made even to-day to maintain our houses of education in

the situation created by these reforms, to alter the new Regulation, the promulgation of which encountered so many difficulties—not to allow its application in those establishments where is trained a youth thoroughly Russian and orthodox? What must every reflecting man think on seeing that this new Regulation, which ought to give to instruction among us the bases recognised by the whole civilised world, is put in operation in provinces of the West; whilst at Moscow even the gymnasia are condemned to languish in a sad state of transition, and, so far as we can judge, seem destined to remain in this state during five whole years, with the prospect at the end of that time of being able to modify or even abrogate the new Regulation?

As to what respects our ecclesiastical schools, not excepting the highest, we can positively aver that Prince Couza would have been perfectly satisfied; he would have found nothing to change in order to attain the end he was pursuing with so much method, decision, and freedom. Here everything Prince Couza could have done has been done, and much even beyond. And now, when the evil is being proved, and the acts of a foreign government unmasked to reveal it, are we making serious efforts to remedy it? What right, then, have we to attack Prince Couza?'

The eminent publicist who so brilliantly conducts the *Moscow Gazette* sets himself to bring out a single point; but if any one will give himself the trouble to read his article with a little attention, he will easily be convinced that the apostrophe with which he concludes it covers not only the classical studies in the seminaries, but every reproach flung at Prince

Couza. This work, which rouses so much indignation in the *Phanar*, and which the *Northern Post* so severely lashes, is after all but a very poor counterfeit of Peter I.'s work.

In presence of M. Katkoff's vigorous reasoning, let us place a few of the conclusions arrived at by M. Wassilieff, in his letter to the Bishop of Nantes.

1. 'The first part of my reply has established that it is not possible, without offending against theology and canon law, to assert that a disciplinary change in a Church is a change in the constitution of that Church.

2. 'I have had the honour of proving to you that the government of a Church by means of a council, is of all forms the most ancient and canonical.

3. 'You have affirmed that the holy Synod was established exclusively by the sovereign of Russia, and for the purpose of enslaving the Church of his empire: I have proved to you that it was otherwise. Relying on facts and authentic documents, I have demonstrated that Peter the Great took part in the establishment of the holy Synod only in a measure proper to a sovereign careful of his public independence—to a Christian sovereign having the right to share in the creation of an ecclesiastical institution, in what concerns its civil and ex-

ternal existence. . . . . I have farther proved, in a solid manner, that the Russian bishops took their due part in the establishment of the holy Synod, both by the counsels they gave for its establishment, and by the drawing up and approval of the organic statute of this permanent council.

4. 'You have affirmed that the approval asked of the Patriarch of Constantinople was too late, and a pure formality: I have given incontestable proofs that, immediately after the convocation of the holy Synod, the sanction of all the Oriental patriarchs was sincerely and respectfully requested; that it was canonically accorded with independence, and with the least possible delay.'*

If Prince Couza, in the leisure afforded him by the instability of human affairs, seeks consolation in the perusal of M. Wassilieff's pamphlet, the page we have just quoted can excite in his heart only the most poignant regrets. Had he but known M. Wassilieff some years sooner, what a theologian, what a canonist, what an advocate might he have found in him! How the learned archpriest would have kept in his place the Patriarch of Constantinople, with his council of deposed and non-deposed patriarchs, and the archimandrite Cleobulus himself! How

* *Discussion,* &c. pp. 50, 51.

he would have shown to the *Northern Post* that it knew not what it was saying! and how he would have obliged M. Katkoff to confess that he was speaking of things he did not understand, when he allowed himself to talk with so much irreverence on the subject of the ecclesiastical schools, even the highest, *i. e.* the academies! M. Wassilieff would even have proved to the Synod that, if his conclusion was reasonable, he had advanced among the grounds of it propositions singularly bold, which could not be sustained without doing violence to theology and canonical law.

We will now leave Prince Couza to his regrets, and M. Wassilieff to the contests with his numerous antagonists, and go at once to the heart of the question.

Here we must carefully distinguish theory from practice. As we have been able, by the numerous documents we have cited, to satisfy ourselves, in a theoretical point of view, the doctrine of the Oriental Church touching the distinction of the two powers and the Church's independence is perfectly correct. Take, for example, M. Wassilieff. He defends the institution of the Synod in Russia, but is convinced that it is the work of the Russian Church herself, and of the œcumenical Church, acting in the plenitude of their liberty and independ-

ence. Peter I., 'tis true, counts there for something, but merely gives his concurrence to the
decisions of the Church. M. Wassilieff also
admits the part assigned to the chief procurator
of the Synod, but in him he sees only a benefactor and servant of this ecclesiastical assembly; and if this servant ever took upon himself
to assume any authority,—if he raised his voice,
if he undertook to counteract the deliberations
of the Synod, or if he so far forgot himself as
to close the discussion and raise the sitting—
he who is so little the president of the Synod
as not to be a member of it,—the learned archpriest would be ready to say to him, 'Sir, you
interfere with what does not concern you. The
most holy assembly, of which you are not a
member, desires to be alone in closing its deliberations: go; when it needs you, it will call
for you.'

The holy Synod invites the bishops holding their nominations of the lay authorities to
confront the 30th canon of the holy Apostles.
Now this canon runs thus: *Si quis episcopus
sæcularibus potestatibus usus ecclesiam per ipsas
obtineat, deponatur et segregetur, et omnes qui
illi communicant.** He is therefore convinced

---

* Εἰ τίς ἐπίσκοπος κυσμίκοις ἀρχοῦσι χρησάμενος, &c. Hefele, vol.
i. p. 183. We have already remarked that the text of this canon
sufficiently proves that it is not of apostolic origin; but it has been
sanctioned by the authority of the Oriental Church, and still has

that, among all the bishops with whom he is in communion, there is not one who has had recourse to the secular power to obtain a bishopric. We need not cite the Patriarch of Constantinople, whose language is very strong. When, then, Catholic or Protestant writers advance that the Russian Church recognises the Russian emperor as its hierarchical head, they are utterly in error. The Russian emperors are laymen, and have no place in the hierarchy. It is true that Paul I., confounding the consecration of emperors with sacerdotal ordination, thought himself a priest. He one day wished to say Mass, and was successfully turned from his purpose only by being reminded that, having been twice married, he was on this account disqualified for the service of the altar. But here was the whim of an individual; although, however, some trace of exaggeration could be found elsewhere* respecting the consecration of the anointed of the Lord and of His Christs.

In the Byzantine Church we find, with respect to the emperors of the lower empire, formularies too obsequious, and a condescension

---

the force of law. 'If any bishop, making use of the secular powers, obtain a church through them, let him be deposed and separated, and all who communicate with him.'

* In the *Office of Orthodoxy*. See Tondini; *The Pope*, &c. pp. 102-103.

which is exaggerated. The doctrine of *the outside bishop** received there too great an extension; but this very expression shows that the emperors are outside the hierarchy, and have no place therein; and it may be said that on this point, as on many others, the doctrine of the Oriental Church has not been altered, her principles have not been sacrificed.

We have spoken here only of theory. If we pass to her practice, we find ourselves in presence of a very different situation. Under the Byzantine emperors, as from the time of the old Tsars of Muscovy, we can verify, on the part of the temporal sovereign, exaggerated pretensions, and encroachments of the lay power on the ecclesiastical domains; but this shows itself more or less everywhere. The Greek Church, like the Russian, can be reproached with a certain softness, a certain want of energy in presence of these pretensions and encroachments of the civil power,—of fits of weakness more or less frequent; but strictly speaking,

---

* Eusebius, in l. iv. c. xxiv. of his *Life of Constantine,* says of the Emperor Constantine : ' Wherefore, when once receiving us (the bishops) at table, he said in our hearing that he also was a bishop, using these words: " You are bishops of those *within* the Church ; but I too have been appointed by God a bishop of those *outside* the Church." And, remembering his words, I observed that he governed all beneath his sway with episcopal solicitude, and urged them by every means in his power to pursue the path of true piety.' (*Trans.*)

all this can be considered as accidental and transitory. Undoubtedly the Tsar Alexis deposed the Patriarch Nicon, but he had recourse to the intervention of a council attended by the Oriental patriarchs. Moreover, this deposition was regarded by contemporaries as a great iniquity. It was one of the first cares of Alexis's son and successor to repair it; and Alexis himself, when dying, overcome by remorse, requested pardon of the deposed patriarch. A violation of a law does not abolish it, and a right is not destroyed because it has been forgotten.

From all these considerations, we hesitate not to say that the doctrine of the Oriental Church nowhere recognises in the prince, we do not say the head of the Universal Church, but not even the head of a particular Church. Must we from this conclude that M. Wassilieff is right, and that the Russian Church, for example, is in possession of its independence? This is not what we wish to say; but to present this delicate and complicated question fully and clearly, we must enter into some detail.

We will begin by examining the nature and extent of the authority assumed by the emperors of Russia, and expressed by the term *autocracy;* and here we specially have in view Peter I. and his successors. We are compelled to admit that they arrogate to themselves an authority that does not belong to them; but let us carefully note, that this follows from the idea which they form of their power, not from the doctrine of the Church of which they are part. They assume the same rights in presence of all Churches and all confessions; and whilst professing to respect the dogmas of all confessions—whether Christian or not—they claim to have the upper hand everywhere in the government of religious as of civil society. Catherine II. very well expressed this idea in her ukase of August 12, 1762, on the goods of the clergy. Speaking of her predecessors, she there says, among other things, that they, ' like all monarchs, received from God *the principal authority in the Church.*' One might fancy he heard the echo of St. Irenæus's voice claiming for the bishops of Rome *potiorem principalitatem.*

Let us now listen to Peter I. as he seeks to justify the establishment of the Synod. ' Monarchs,' says he, ' although they possess an absolute power, since, according to the Divine precept, an unhesitating obedience is due to them, employ councillors, not only for better getting at the truth, but also for stopping the calumnies of perverse men, who would ascribe this or that order of the sovereign to violence and passion, rather than to the right and legitimate cause. This applies still more to ecclesiastical government, which is *deprived of an absolute and independent power*, since domination over the clergy is forbidden even to those who hold the helm of the Church.'[*]

Confounding, by a clever sophism, the *spirit of domination* with *authority*, Peter laid it down that those who are at the helm of the Church, viz. the bishops, metropolitans, patriarchs, &c. —in a word, the pastors—are without independent authority. According to him, supreme authority in Church government, as in civil society, belongs to the sovereign, whom all ought in everything to obey without murmuring. This settled, he finds it convenient that the sovereign should be surrounded with ecclesiastical councillors, to aid him in governing the Church; but they are only councillors, and the authority intrusted to them they hold of him, and are accountable for its proper exer-

---

[*] ... ' Monarchæ etiam, quamvis absoluta gaudeant potentia, quippe quibus, secundum divinum præceptum, obedientia citra reclamationem debetur, a consiliariis tamen, non eo solum fine, ut in veritate investiganda felicius proficiant, sed ne homines quoque pervicaces hoc aut illud per vim potius et ex affectu, quam jure et legitime a monarchis præcipi calumnientur, minime abhorrent. Id autem magis quadrat in ecclesiasticum regimen, utpote *absoluta et independente potentia destitutum* adeo ut ipsi quoque Ecclesiæ gubernacula tenenti dominatio in clerum denegetur.' (*Statutum Canonicum Petri Magni*, Petropoli, 1785, pp. 11, 12.)

cise to him. These principles show themselves, under all forms, at the bottom of Russian legislation. Thence springs the right of naming and displacing bishops, and the complete and absolute dependence of the whole hierarchy on the sovereign. Thence, moreover, in matters ecclesiastical, the concentration of the exercise of legislative authority in the hands of the emperor. No ecclesiastical authority in the Russian clergy, however exalted, can promulgate, modify, suspend, or abrogate any ecclesiastical law, without the emperor's consent and sanction. On the contrary, it suffices, in order that a law of the emperor's on an ecclesiastical matter may become obligatory, that it have received the countersign of the Synod. This countersign would have the force of a guarantee, if it emanated from an independent authority; but the organisation and mechanism of the Synod being such as we have described them, it is simply a formality.

Not only, as we have said, is it in respect of the national and official Church that the Russian government claims this authority, but also in respect of all religions. Hence the insurmountable difficulties in the construction, and above all in the enforcement, of concordats with the Holy See. From the point of view of the Russian government, the supreme author-

ity over the Catholic Church in Russia sub-
stantially resides in the emperor. He is quite
willing that the Mass be said in Latin, that the
Filioque be inserted in the symbol, that un-
leavened bread be used, that the communion
be in one kind only; but these concessions
made, he sincerely believes he has the right to
rule the Catholic Church in his States, the
Protestant and Armenian, just as the national
Church. He applies the same principles to
Jews, Mussulmans, and Buddhists; and this
equality of all religions before imperial supremacy constitutes what is in Russia called
toleration. As is witnessed, a perpetual misunderstanding and radical opposition exists
between the Catholic Church and the Russian
autocracy.

The two powers speak a different language;
the same words in their lips have not the same
signification. For our part, we are ready to
admit that there may be in Russia those who
persecute the Catholic Church, and labour to
destroy it, whilst quite persuaded that, with a
certain degree of good faith, they are the most
tolerant men in the world.

We can now see how we are to understand
the position maintained by M. Wassilieff, viz.
'The first part of my reply has proved to you

that it is not permitted, without doing violence
to theology and canon law, to affirm that a
change of discipline in a Church is a change
of the constitution of that Church' (op. cit.
p. 50). M. Wassilieff is here speaking of the
establishment of the Synod. What he calls a
change of discipline is not only a change in the
constitution of the Church, but the destruction
of this constitution, the substitution of the imperial power for the ecclesiastical in the government of the Church.

We cited above the formula of oath taken
by the members of the Synod. It will be recollected that in it they declared that the emperor is supreme judge in that assembly. M.
Wassilieff gives himself much trouble to assign
to this inconvenient text an acceptable sense.
He supposes the formula of oath taken by the
members to be composed of two parts; in the
first, an oath of fidelity to the Church is taken;
in the second, to the sovereign. He thence
concludes that 'the words quoted relate to the
members of the Holy Synod only in their
quality of subjects, of dignitaries of the State,
of members of a mixed assembly, having a
double character—religious and civil.' We
have already observed that the members of the
Synod do not recognise the emperor as their

judge—an avowal not asked of them—but as judge of the Synod, *supremum hujusce collegii judicem*, which admits of no equivocation whatever. This means that an appeal can be made from the Synod to the emperor, and to him only. Now, the Synod is the highest authority existing in the Russian Church; to it all owe submission and obedience; it holds the place of patriarch. According to the letter of Jeremiah, Patriarch of Constantinople, it has a power equal to that of each of the four patriarchates; and yet it is under the emperor's jurisdiction. After this it is difficult to dispute the emperor's exercise of authority over the Church.

When Peter I. caused his son to be tried and condemned, before the sentence was pronounced he requested a consultation with the clergy. We have the account of this: it is dated June 18th, 1718, and is signed by eight bishops and six archimandrites, of whom several are found among the signataries of the ecclesiastical statute and the first members of the Synod. We there read this passage: 'Who has made us judges of those who exercise authority over us? How can the members instruct the head, which ought to instruct and govern them?' The members are the bishops; the head is the Tsar; and from beginning to end of this remarkable document the members speak like bishops.*

M. Wassilieff does not wish it to be said that the Russian Church is subject to the civil power; he is right. It can be said that the Church of Constantinople is subject to the sultan; but in spite of the oppression burdening her, we yet recognise in her a distinct society, with her own spirit, legislation, traditions, and magistrates: she wears chains, but still lives. In Russia the situation is wholly different. The Church has no life of its own: in everything she receives impulse from without. The clergy wear mitres and copes; this is the one respect distinguishing them from the other functionaries of the State. The Russian Church is not *subjected*, she is *absorbed* by the State: she is an inert instrument, a body without a soul.

Between her and the old Russian Church there is no identity; they are two things en-

---

* A characteristic detail confirms our view. In the annual report published by the chief procurator of the Synod, mention is made of the new privileges just granted to the bishops. Henceforth they will be able to absent themselves from their dioceses for eight days, on simply giving notice to the Synod, and without waiting for its permission; with the Synod's authorisation, they will be able to absent themselves for twenty-nine days; for a longer absence the imperial decision must be asked. How clearly do we discern the hierarchy through this arrangement: for eight days, the bishop; for a month, the Synod; for six weeks or three months, the emperor. This is at once ridiculous and odious.

tirely distinct, whose resemblance is altogether external.

Peter I. effected a religious revolution comparable only to that accomplished in England by Henry VIII. and Elizabeth; he did in Russia what Prince Couza attempted in Roumania. To be convinced of this we have but to reproduce an extract from the annual report recently presented to the emperor by Count Dmitri Tolstoy, the present chief procurator of the Synod. See, first of all, how he appreciates the acts of the old Hospodar: 'Prince Couza,' says the report, 'who evidently proposed to draw the people into union with the Latin Church, and separate them from the patriarchal see of Constantinople, proclaimed, arbitrarily and in contempt of the laws, the Roumain Church to be independent of all foreign ecclesiastical authority. At the same time he stripped this Church, feigned to be independent, of the degree of independence always enjoyed in her internal administration. The General Synod created by the Hospodar's decree, and destined to centralise in its own bosom the high administration of ecclesiastical affairs, has been placed in complete dependence on the laity. The right to convoke and dissolve this assembly was assumed by the Hospodar; the choice of bishops and metropolitans he confided to his ministers, reserving to himself their confirmation. The ties of dependence binding the clergy to the diocesan bishop were relaxed; houses of instruction subjected to a reform which deprived aspirants to the priesthood of the possibility of receiving a sufficient theological education; to those who felt themselves called to the religious life, such excessively troublesome conditions were opposed as almost to amount to a bar to their embracing the monastic state; civil marriage was recognised as legal, &c.'—This obviously is the counterpart of Peter I.'s acts. The chief procurator is naturally averse to admit it; and hence he sets himself to indicate the difference. In his reply to the Patriarch of Constantinople, he says, in the same report, the holy Synod has set the facts in their true light. Thus did Prince Couza support himself on an error as to the Russian patriarch having been replaced by a Synod, in virtue of the will of the emperor Peter I., and as to our method of nominating bishops. It has been shown that the establishment of the Synod took place with the benediction of all the Oriental patriarchs; that in Russia, even now, the bishops select the candidates for the episcopate, and that 'tis only *after* this selection that one of the candidates is confirmed by the supreme authority (*i. e.* the emperor's).

In what, then, consists the difference, according to Count Dmitri Tolstoy? First, in this, that the order of things founded by Peter I. received the sanction of the Oriental patriarchs, and, secondly, that the episcopal nominations are sanctioned by the choice of the Synod. We willingly recognise that this double difference would be capital, if in either case there were anything more than a formality, an empty image. But in presence of the facts, it is impossible not to see that, if external forms seem to have been preserved, in reality everything has been changed. Prince Couza's General Synod had even more independence than Peter's governing Synod: events have proved it. Count Tolstoy says that the Hospodar arrogated to himself the right of convoking and dissolving the General Synod: we have shown that the Russian Synod can oppose no resistance to the emperor's wishes, since it depends on him to call to or dismiss from the Synod whom he please; and none knows better than the chief procurator, unless it be the Synod itself, that the emperor is not scrupulous in his choice of bishops.

Now as to the approval given by the Oriental patriarchs to the establishment of the Synod. We are well aware that there was a sham-council in Russia and a sham-approba-

tion on the part of the Oriental patriarchs;
but it is certain that neither the council nor
the patriarchs freely pronounced themselves.
In an article published September 8th, 1862, by
the *Ecclesiastical Talk*,* under the signature of
Father Athanasius, it is said, in reference to
this council: 'Beyond a doubt those who sat
in it did not consent, all, and at once, to Peter's
proposition, . . . but the Tsar's will, sustained
by a few ecclesiastics, gained the day' (p. 221).

Now, this article, although it bears visible
traces of the author's embarrassment, is on the
whole favourable to Peter's innovation, and is
clothed with the approbation of the ecclesiastical censorship: the acknowledgment, therefore,
has importance. What Father Athanasius
says of Peter's council, we in our turn will say
of the approbation of the Patriarch of Constantinople: 'tis a pure formality, which after the
fact could not be refused to the puissant emperor who had vanquished Charles XII. and
whose hosts inspired the Turks with terror,
and the Greeks with hope. We may well
suppose that if the patriarch had been consulted at an opportune time, and especially if
he had not had to deal with a prince whose
power bore with so terrible a weight in the
councils of the *Phanar*, he would not have al-

* Духовная беседа.

lowed an innovation, so unheard of in the annals of the Church, to pass without a protest.
The approbation, however, does not legitimise
Peter's work; it proves only the abasement of
the Greek Church. Moreover, we have shown
by dates that this approval was given only
after the fact; no uneasiness was felt at the
time of the institution of the Synod, nor was
any dreamt of until the whole thing was done.
This revolution was the work of Peter solely,
without the concurrence of the Oriental Church.

Finally, it was not the first time that the
Tsars requested any concession and signature
of the Eastern patriarchs: there were precedents. When the Ukraine Church was severed
from the Patriarchate of Constantinople, to be
subjected to that of Moscow (1685), the whole
matter was directly negotiated and concluded
between the interested parties, without any intervention on the part of the Bysantine Church.
The hetman Samoïlovich, fearing excommunication, demanded that the consent of the Patriarch of Constantinople should be obtained.
The latter, named James, and Dositheus, Patriarch of Jerusalem, began by refusing, declar-
ing that to consent would be contrary to the
rules laid down by the holy fathers. The Russian envoys then addressed themselves to the
Grand Vizier, who declared himself charmed

to do anything agreeable to the Tsar, and that he would at once issue the necessary orders to the patriarchs. Immediately afterwards, Dositheus found a canon which he had not known of, and which rendered perfectly lawful what had hitherto been impossible. In the interval James had been deposed, and replaced by Dionysius, who had before filled the see of Constantinople. Dionysius delivered to the Russian envoys all the necessary papers, and received in exchange two hundred pieces of gold and forty skins of sable; Dositheus also had two hundred pieces of gold. Dionysius, besides, demanded that money should be sent to all the episcopal signitaries of the acts, as was done in the time of the Tsar Feodore Ivanovich, whose liberality was extended to all the bishops taking part in the erection of the Moscow patriarchate (Solovieff, *History of Russia*, vol. xiv. p. 35). 'Twas therefore the Grand Vizier's will and Russia's gold that determined the consent of the patriarchs; motives of the same kind caused the official recognition of the Synod.

That Peter I. was more skilful than Prince Couza, we readily recognise; but this is not the question. Nor is it a question as to whether, in the organisation of the Russian Church in 1721, imperial omnipotence showed itself openly, or prudently veiled itself in a simulated garb. Was the Church in 1721 stripped of her legitimate authority, or not? This is the question. Prince Couza in Roumania tried to usurp this authority. We admit it, and subscribe most cheerfully to the judgment passed by the Patriarch of Constantinople, the Russian Synod, the chief procurator of the Synod, and the *Northern Post.* But when they come to tell us that in Russia the Church has remained independent, that it preserved all its rightful authority, we cannot accept this language, but demonstrate the contrary by facts.

It is very easy to understand that a Church thus enslaved ought to find herself in a state of isolation with respect to the other Churches. This M. Katkoff has justly observed. Speaking of the different Churches of the Oriental communion, he says they have no bond among them, no settled relationship; they are not parts of a whole. This would require a common organisation, which would bind together their scattered members and make of them one body. There can be no unity where there is no centre. Let this centre be a council, a commission, or an individual, a centre is indispensable. Now, this centre does not exist.

Has it, at least, been sought to supply the place of these regular relations by exchange of ideas? Thus, for example, the different states of Europe are perfectly independent of one another,—they do not even form a confederation; yet they maintain among themselves diplomatic relations and correspondence; they have representatives accredited one to another. In the Oriental Church there is nothing of the kind. The Russian emperor is in closer relations with the emperor of China than is the Synod with the Patriarch of Constantinople; and the letters exchanged in 1865, on the subject of the Roumain Church, are perhaps the first instance of a common consultation for nearly one hundred and fifty years of the Synod's existence.

It has justly been said that the different Churches of the Oriental communion may be compared to the defunct Germanic Confederation, less the Frankfort Diet. How is it that they have never succeeded in constituting a kind of ecclesiastical diet, by which all correspondence should be ultimatumed, and which should serve as a bond to all the Churches, which now have become so completely estranged from one another? This long state of isolation, in spite of all stereotyped phrases about the immobility and unchangeableness of the Oriental Churches, could not continue without the introduction of new situations, new customs, and new points of view; hence arose differences, as M. Katkoff very well observes, very perceptible, and even very profound. If among the clergy or laity in Russia there were people who would take religious affairs to heart, and feel a serious interest in the Church to which they belong, these differences between the several Churches, which pretend to form but one, would become the subject of conscientious study and of graver discussions. But it is not so. On the contrary, we behold the strangest indifference, and apathy the most complete. It needed that an Englishman* should call attention to the very different manner in which the Constantinopolitan and Russian Churches view the conditions necessary to the validity of baptism.

At Constantinople baptism by immersion only is admitted as valid. The consequence is that, in the eyes of that Church, Latin Catholics and Protestants are not Christians. Should a member of either of them request to be received into the Greek Church, she will impose on him the obligation to be baptised. The doctrine of the Russian Church is more liberal: in her view baptism by immersion is a matter of rite, and not of dogma. She recognises

* W. Palmer, Esq., M.A., of Magdalen College, Oxon, the author of *The Patriarch and the Tsar,—Replies of the humble Nicon*, &c.

Latins and Protestants as validly baptised, and consequently as Christians; and when the other necessary conditions distinguish candidates, they are admitted into the Church free from the obligation of a new baptism, as was lately seen in the case of the Princess Dagmar. If the opinion of the Greeks were rightly founded, this princess, as also all the Russian empresses and the spouses of the grand dukes, would not be Christians. The question is certainly not without importance; and yet the Patriarch of Constantinople and the Russian Synod are not agreed on it.*

This state of separation, it is true, existed when the Russian Church had a patriarch at her head; but since the creation of the Synod, since the absorption of the Russian Church by

* The *Ecclesiastical Talk* of Sept. 17, 1866, was seeking for a means of reconciling on this point the Greek and Russian Churches. Nothing is stranger than the idea it has entertained. If we are to believe the *Eccl. Talk*, the Greek Church fully admits the validity of baptism otherwise than by immersion, but has been obliged to exact a new baptism from those Latins seeking admission into her bosom, in order to draw deeper a line of demarcation between Greeks and Latins, from fear of a reconciliation; and to this end has imagined nothing better than to make the Greeks believe that the Latins were not Christians. We should never dare to attribute to the Greek Church such a proceeding. Lying, calumny, profanation of a sacrament that cannot be repeated,—all this, according to the *Ecclesiastical Talk*, the Greek Church would knowingly and willingly do! Reading this, we cannot believe our eyes. And this journal is published by the Ecclesiastical Academy of St. Petersburg, under the eyes and with the approbation of the Synod.

the State, the situation has been singularly aggravated. Suppose an independent patriarch to be to-day (1872) at the head of the Russian Church, the facility and rapidity of communication, the close connection into which the interests of people the most distant enter,—everything will lead him into relations with his colleague of Constantinople. Nothing is more simple than to write a letter; a few days after comes the reply, and correspondence is established. Should any matter necessitating more complete explanation arise, he will send one of his priests to Constantinople. Instead of this, for the Synod to write a letter the emperor's authorisation is previously necessary; then, to produce unanimity, and to agree on the drawing up and on the choice of expressions, long deliberations must still ensue. The drawing up itself must be submitted to the ministry; difficulties are multiplied; nor will the letter ultimately be dispatched, unless it be in perfect harmony with the minister's instructions to the ambassador. The Synod will take no step without being checked by a thousand restraints. In vain it holds the pen; its writings will not emanate from it, but from the government. But the government may wish to gain over the patriarch to its interests, without allowing him to meddle with anything whatever, even as a councillor, on the affairs of the Russian Church.

So also as to the relations of the Synod with the Russian bishops. Once admit the hypothesis of a patriarch, and nothing is easier than an intimate, familiar, and cordial correspondence between him and the bishops. From time to time the bishops come to visit him, open their hearts to him, share with him their embarrassments, the difficulties they encounter, the troubles they feel; and so a half-hour's conversation can terminate an affair which would have demanded months of correspondence. With the Synod, naught but bureaucracy, papers passing from the chancery of the consistory to that of the Synod, a mere exchange of formulas with signatures, — what can issue from thence?

Suppose, however, that the bishop has, with great difficulty, obtained permission to come to Petersburg, he visits one after another all the members of the Synod, explains his business, and succeeds (a thing unheard of) in bringing them all to his opinion,—the opposition of the chancery, and especially that of the chief procurator, can stop everything. It would seem as though a system had been expressly invented to multiply instead of taking away difficulties, and to prevent all action. Once caught in this network, the bishops and clergy lose all power of judging the situation. They do not satisfy themselves as to the causes of the servitude which enthralls them. They do not understand that the root of all the mischief is the absorption of the Church by the State.

We here touch the heart of the question.

Of what use are all commissions and inquiries on the situation of the clergy? They never will tell the truth; they never can, even if it be that those who compose them have inwardly some suspicion of it. The root of the evil, we repeat, is the State's absorption of the Church. Leviteism and the invasion of bureaucracy into ecclesiastical administration are doubtless very great evils, but they are the necessary consequences of the fundamental evil; and the knot in which all the mischievous fibres of the system gather is the Synod. The remedy is the abolition of the Synod. This should be the aim of every effort, the *delenda est Carthago* of every discourse.

The only men in Russia who understand this are the *Rascolniks.* ' I neither recognise absolutely nor countenance your Synod and the clergy of your Church,' said one of these sectaries (Kelsieff, vol. i. p. 220). Another rascolnik of Yaroslaff said to Count Steinbock, ' The Greco - Russian religion is a profane worldly religion; it is not based on a true and sincere conviction; it is a government instrument for maintaining order and the worship of earthly authority.'

This terrestrial authority is designated *Antichrist:* 'The seal of Antichrist, say they, is subordination to its authority; 'tis the observance, in Christ's name, of laws made in the spirit of *Antichrist;* 'tis the contempt, the enslavement of the Church' (Kelsieff, 4th Book, pp. 327-329, London, 1862). These poor people are doubtless coarse and ignorant, but they are sound in judgment. They have seen where the source and principle of all the evils really are; long ago they drew their conclusions from the premises put forward by the Patriarch of Constantinople against Prince Couza; they applied the canons he cited.

Here is the Synod of Russia, which in 1866 recalls the apostolic canon, in virtue of which a bishop guilty of having had recourse to the secular powers for his nomination is deposed and excommunicated, with all who communicate with him. In thus speaking, the Synod justifies all the rascolniks, who do not wish to hear anything of communion with it. The existence of the Synod is the true cause of rascolnism. Suppose the Russian Church independent, and the clergy a little educated, a quarter of a century will not pass before the return of the Staroveres to the Church's communion.

To whatever side we turn our gaze,—the rascol rending the Russian Church, the isolation of this Church with respect to other Oriental Churches, Leviteism, the encroachment of bureaucracy,—we perceive only consequences of the absorption of the Church which the State has effected by means of the Synod. The end will be the conviction that the reform necessary and indispensable in the bosom of the Russian Church is the abolition of the Synod. From this consequence there is no escape.

Must, then, the patriarch be reëstablished? We will say neither Yes nor No. An independent patriarch at the head of the whole Russian Church would be invested with such a power, and afford so few guarantees, that we fully apprehend the fears which would insure the rejection of this project. Besides, there would always exist a fear lest he should become an instrument in the hands of power, or even a spiritual emperor, before whom the temporal emperor, the state itself, and all the populations foreign to the national Church, would have to be effaced.

What, then, is to be done? If a patriarch is wished at any price, he must himself be subject to a higher authority: we have named the Pope. If it is not wished to have a patriarch residing in the country, the example set by all Catholic nations should be followed, and the authority of the Pope—the first of the patriarchs—be recognised. There exist no other means of having a Church that is free without being factious, and that yields obedience to the laws without suffering enslavement.

THE END.